3⁰⁰
f

D1411474

The Observer's Pocket Series

AIRCRAFT

The Observer Books

A POCKET REFERENCE SERIES
COVERING NATURAL HISTORY, TRANSPORT,
THE ARTS ETC

Natural History

BIRDS
BIRDS' EGGS
BUTTERFLIES
LARGER MOTHS
COMMON INSECTS
WILD ANIMALS
ZOO ANIMALS
WILD FLOWERS
GARDEN FLOWERS
FLOWERING TREES
  AND SHRUBS
CACTI
TREES
GRASSES
FERNS
COMMON FUNGI
LICHENS
POND LIFE
FRESHWATER FISHES
SEA FISHES
SEA AND SEASHORE
GEOLOGY
ASTRONOMY
WEATHER
CATS
DOGS
HORSES AND PONIES

Transport

AIRCRAFT
AUTOMOBILES
COMMERCIAL VEHICLES
SHIPS
MANNED SPACEFLIGHT

The Arts etc

ARCHITECTURE
CATHEDRALS
CHURCHES
HERALDRY
FLAGS
PAINTING
MODERN ART
SCULPTURE
FURNITURE
MUSIC
POSTAGE STAMPS

Sport

ASSOCIATION FOOTBALL
CRICKET

Cities

LONDON

The Observer's Book of
AIRCRAFT

COMPILED BY
WILLIAM GREEN

WITH SILHOUETTES BY
DENNIS PUNNETT

DESCRIBING 158 AIRCRAFT
WITH 278 ILLUSTRATIONS

1973 Edition

FREDERICK WARNE & CO LTD
FREDERICK WARNE & CO INC
LONDON · NEW YORK

© FREDERICK WARNE & CO LTD
LONDON, ENGLAND
1973

Twenty-second Edition 1973

LIBRARY OF CONGRESS CATALOG CARD NO: 57–4425

ISBN 0 7232 1514 6

Printed in Great Britain

INTRODUCTION TO THE 1973 EDITION

Shortly before this edition of *The Observer's Book of Aircraft*—the 22nd annual volume—was passed for press a ceasefire was finally arranged in Vietnam and a quasi-peace restored after years of terrible warfare in which the aeroplane had played a major role. It would be idle to suppose that the uneasy peace reigning at the time of writing in this corner of South-East Asia will result in any radical reduction in the tempo of combat aircraft development and redeployment of resources to civil aircraft research, and it may be assumed that the roughly 50–50 mix of military and civil aeroplanes presented in this edition will remain a fairly constant ratio in the years immediately ahead.

The contribution of the Vietnam conflict to the present combat aircraft development scene has undoubtedly been formidable, "Vietnam thinking" sharing with cost considerations responsibility for a new generation of "less sophisticated" warplanes, such as the Fairchild A-10 close support and attack aeroplane, which, having made its début last year, was selected by the USAF for further development after competitive evaluation. "Vietnam thinking" is also influencing the development of new "lightweight" fighters, such as the General Dynamics YF-16 and Northrop YF-17 which may be expected to make their appearance in the 1974 edition, while the ability to tote offensive stores has become *de rigueur* for new instructional aircraft, be they the simplest *ab initio* trainer, such as New Zealand's CT-4 Airtrainer, or basic/advanced trainers, such as the Franco-German Alpha jet, both of which appear for the first time in the pages of this edition.

Despite the gradual political thaw between East and West there is as yet no concrete evidence of serious reduction in the tempo of combat aircraft development for both offence and defence. In the former category a supersonic variable-geometry strategic bomber dubbed *Backfire* by NATO is allegedly entering quantity production, although insufficient substantive evidence concerning the appearance of this advanced warplane was available at the time of closing for press to warrant its inclusion in this edition of *The Observer's Book of Aircraft*. The US counterpart of *Backfire*, the North American Rockwell B-1, is scheduled to commence its test programme next year and will duly take its place in the 1974 edition. The latest in air-superiority fighter ̓esign to reach the hardware stage is represented in the following ̓ges by the F-15 Eagle, and the growing importance attached to ̓orne early warning is indicated by the appearance in this edition ̓e Tupolev AEW aeroplane code-named *Moss* and the Boeing ̓ 37D, forerunner of the E-3A.

̓ in past years, all data have been updated and all general-̓ ̓ement silhouettes thoroughly checked and, where necessary, ̓ or replaced.

WILLIAM GREEN

AERITALIA-AERMACCHI AM-3C

Country of Origin: Italy.
Type: Battlefield surveillance and forward air control aircraft.
Power Plant: One 340 hp Piaggio-built Avco Lycoming GSO-480-B1B6 six-cylinder horizontally-opposed engine.
Performance: (At 3,307 lb/1 500 kg) Max. speed, 161 mph (260 km/h) at sea level, 173 mph (278 km/h) at 8,000 ft (2 440 m); max. cruise, 153 mph (246 km/h) at 8,000 ft (2 440 m); max. range (with 30 min reserves), 615 mls (990 km); initial climb, 1,378 ft/min (7,0 m/sec).
Weights: Empty equipped, 2,548 lb (1 156 kg); normal loaded, 3,307 lb (1 500 kg); max. take-off, 3,858 lb (1 750 kg).
Armament: Four underwing hardpoints for various ordnance loads. Two inner hardpoints stressed for 375 lb (170 kg) and two outer hardpoints stressed for 200 lb (91 kg). Armament options include four LAU-32A or Matra 181 rocket launchers, 12 80-mm SURA rockets, two Nord AS.11 missiles, two 7,62-mm Minigun pods, or two 250-lb (113,4-kg) and two 200-lb (91-kg) bombs.
Accommodation: Pilot and co-pilot in tandem with optional third seat aft.
Status: First of two flying prototypes flown May 12, 196_ followed by second on August 22, 1968. First product_ example commenced test programme mid-1972 with in_ deliveries (against order for 40 from South Africa) sche_ for early 1973.
Notes: Three ordered by Rwanda and order for 20 _ in training role anticipated from Italian Army.

6

AERITALIA-AERMACCHI AM-3C

Dimensions: Span, 41 ft $5\frac{1}{3}$ in (12,64 m); length, 29 ft $5\frac{1}{2}$ in (8,98 m); height, 8 ft 11 in (2,72 m); wing area, 219·15 sq ft (20,36 m²).

AERITALIA (FIAT) G.91Y

Country of Origin: Italy.
Type: Single-seat light tactical fighter-bomber and reconnaissance aircraft.
Power Plant: Two 2,725 lb (1 236 kg) dry and 4,080 lb (1 850 kg) reheat General Electric J85-GE-13A turbojets.
Performance: Max. speed, 690 mph (1 110 km/h) or Mach 0·9 at sea level, 670 mph (1 080 km/h) or Mach 0·95 at 32,810 ft (10 000 m); range cruise at 490 ft (150 m), 390 mph (630 km/h); typical tactical radius for lo-lo-lo mission with 2,910-lb (1 320-kg) payload, 240 mls (385 km); ferry range with two 176 Imp gal (800 l) auxiliary tanks and 10% reserves, 2,110 mls (3 400 km); max. initial climb, 17,000 ft/min (86,36 m/sec); service ceiling, 41,000 ft (12 500 m).
Weights: Empty, 8,598 lb (3 900 kg); normal max. take-off, 17,196 lb (7 800 kg); max. overload take-off, 19,180 lb (8 700 kg).
Armament: Two 30-mm DEFA 552 cannon. Four underwing stores stations for max. of 4,000 lb (1 814 kg) ordnance.
Status: First of two prototypes flown December 27, 1966, and first of 20 pre-production aircraft flown July 1968. Delivery of 55 production aircraft to Italian Air Force scheduled for completion during 1973.
Notes: Prototype of a modified version with more advanced avionics (including Saab bombing computer) for evaluation by Switzerland was flown on October 16, 1970. This, the G.91YS, features two additional underwing stores points each able to carry a Sidewinder AAM. The G.91YT is a projected two-seat training version.

AERITALIA (FIAT) G.91Y

Dimensions: Span, 29 ft 6½ in (9,01 m); length, 38 ft 3½ in (11,67 m); height, 14 ft 6⅓ in (4,43 m); wing area, 195·149 sq ft (18,13 m²).

AERITALIA (FIAT) G.222

Country of Origin: Italy.

Type: General-purpose military transport.

Power Plant: Two 2,970 shp General Electric CT64-820 turboprops. (Production) Two 3,400 shp T64-P4D turboprops.

Performance: (Estimated with T64-P4D engines) Max. speed, 329 mph (530 km/h) at sea level; normal cruise, 273 mph (440 km/h) at 14,750 ft (4 500 m); range with 11,025-lb (5 000-kg) payload, 1,920 mls (3 250 km), with max. fuel, 3,262 mls (5 250 km); max. initial climb rate, 1,890 ft/min (9,6 m/sec).

Weights: Empty, 29,320 lb (13 300 kg); empty equipped, 32,408 lb (14 700 kg); max. take-off, 57,320 lb (26 000 kg).

Accommodation: Flight crew of three or four and seats for 44 fully-equipped troops or 40 paratroops. Alternative loads include 36 casualty stretchers, two jeep-type vehicles or equivalent freight.

Status: First of two prototypes flown July 18, 1970, followed by second prototype on July 22, 1971, and work had begun on six pre-production examples at the beginning of 1973. An order for 44 aircraft for the Italian Air Force was placed on July 28, 1972, and it is anticipated that deliveries of the G.222 will be made 1974–75.

Notes: Prototypes powered by CT64-820 turboprops and unpressurised, but the programmed production model will have uprated T64-P4D turboprops and provision for pressurisation. The G.222 is intended as a successor to some of the Italian Air Force's ageing Fairchild C-119 transports.

AERITALIA (FIAT) G.222

Dimensions: Span, 94 ft 5¾ in (28,80 m); length, 74 ft 5½ in (22,70 m); height, 32 ft 1¾ in (9,80 m); wing area, 970·9 sq ft (90,2 m²).

AERMACCHI M.B.326K

Country of Origin: Italy.

Type: Single-seat operational trainer and close-support aircraft.

Power Plant: One 4,000 lb (1 814 kg) Rolls-Royce Viper 632-43 turbojet.

Performance: (Estimated) Max. speed without external stores, 550 mph (885 km/h) at 19,685 ft (6 000 m); max. cruise, 497 mph (800 km/h); ferry range with two 90 Imp. gal. (409 l) underwing auxiliary tanks, 1,400 mls (2 250 km).

Weights: Empty equipped, 6,298 lb (2 857 kg); loaded (clean), 9,678 lb (4 390 kg); max., 12,000 lb (5 443 kg).

Armament: Two 30-mm DEFA or Aden cannon with 150 rpg. Six underwing stores stations of which four stressed for loads up to 1,000 lb (453,5 kg) and two for loads up to 750 lb (340 kg). Max. external ordnance load of 4,500 lb (2 040 kg).

Status: First prototype M.B.326K flown August 22, 1970 with Viper 540 turbojet and second prototype with Viper 632 flown May 21, 1971. Flight test programme completed during 1972 with production commencing early 1973.

Notes: M.B.326K is a single-seat dual-purpose derivative of the two-seat M.B.326G with the 3,410 lb (1 547 kg) Viper 540 turbojet (see 1970 edition). Apart from a more powerful turbojet, built-in cannon armament and a single-seat cockpit, the M.B.326K embodies some local strengthening of the forward fuselage structure, a high-flotation undercarriage, and provision for armour protection. Assembly in South Africa is scheduled to commence in 1974.

12

AERMACCHI M.B.326K

Dimensions: Span (over tip tanks), 35 ft $6\frac{3}{4}$ in (10,84 m); length, 34 ft $10\frac{7}{8}$ in (10,64 m); height, 12 ft $1\frac{3}{4}$ in (3,70 m); wing area, 207·958 sq ft (19,32 m²).

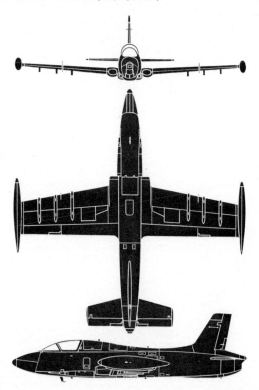

AERO L 39

Country of Origin: Czechoslovakia.

Type: Tandem two-seat basic and advanced trainer.

Power Plant: One 3,307 lb (1 500 kg) Walter Titan (Ivchenko AI-25V) turbofan.

Performance: Max. speed, 379 mph (610 km/h) at sea level, 454 mph (730 km/h) at 16,400 ft (5 000 m); range on internal fuel with 5% reserves, 680 mls (1 100 km), with tip-tanks and no reserves, 930 mls (1 500 km); initial climb, 3,740 ft/min (19 m/sec).

Weights: Empty, 6,283 lb (2 850 kg); normal loaded, 8,377 lb (3 800 kg); max. take-off, 9,480 lb (4 300 kg).

Status: First of five flying prototypes flown on November 4, 1968, and first of pre-production batch of 10 aircraft joined test programme during 1971 with full production commencing in 1972. Orders for 700 L 39s had been placed by beginning of 1971, including 300 for the Soviet Union. Czechoslovak Air Force expected to receive up to 300 during 1973–75.

Notes: The L 39 is intended as a successor for the L 29 Delfin, and a 3,968-lb (1 800-kg) version of the Titan (AI-25VM) with a two-stage fan is under development for the production model. An afterburning Titan of some 4,410 lb (2 000 kg) is being developed for a light strike version of the L 39. This model will feature wing hard points for gun pods, ASMs and bombs, and is intended primarily for sale in Africa and Asia.

14

AERO L 39

Dimensions: Span, 29 ft $10\frac{3}{4}$ in (9,11 m); length, 39 ft $10\frac{2}{3}$ in (12,12 m); height, 14 ft $4\frac{1}{4}$ in (4,38 m); wing area, 202·4 sq ft (18,8 m²).

AÉROSPATIALE SN 601 CORVETTE

Country of Origin: France.

Type: Light business executive transport.

Power Plant: Two 2,310 lb (1 048 kg) Pratt & Whitney JT15D-4 turbofans.

Performance: Max. cruise at 12,125 lb (5 500 kg), 495 mph (796 km/h) at 29,530 ft (9 000 m), at 13,448 lb (6 100 kg), 483 mph (778 km/h) at 25,000 ft (7 620 m); econ. cruise, 385 mph (620 km/h) at 36,090 ft (11 000 m); max. range on internal fuel, 913 mls (1 470 km) at econ. cruise with reserves for 45 min hold at 5,000 ft (1 520 m), with optional 77 Imp gal (350 l) wingtip tanks, 1,520 mls (2 445 km); max. climb, 3,000 ft/min (15,25 m/sec).

Weights: Empty equipped, 7,985 lb (3 622 kg); max. take-off, 13,448 lb (6 100 kg).

Accommodation: Crew of one or two on flight deck plus 4–6 passengers in executive version. Standard arrangements for 8, 10 or 12 passengers and aeromedical arrangement for three stretchers and two medical attendants.

Status: Prototype (SN 600) flown July 16, 1970, followed by first of two pre-series aircraft (SN 601) on December 20, 1972. First of initial production series of five to fly by October 1973. Second production series of 13 to follow with initial customer deliveries early 1974. Production rate of two per month scheduled for late 1974.

Notes: The SN 601 Corvette differs from the original SN 600 in having an aerodynamically refined and lengthened fuselage, redesigned vertical tail surfaces and uprated engines.

AÉROSPATIALE SN 601 CORVETTE

Dimensions: Span, 41 ft 11⅞ in (12,80 m), with tip tanks, 43 ft 5¼ in (13,24 m); length, 45 ft 4 in (13,82 m); height, 13 ft 10 in (4,23 m); wing area, 236·8 sq ft (22,00 m²).

AÉROSPATIALE N 262C FRÉGATE

Country of Origin: France.

Type: Light short-range feederliner.

Power Plant: Two 1,360 shp Turboméca Bastan VIIA turboprops.

Performance: Max. speed, 260 mph (418 km/h); max. cruise, 254 mph (408 km/h) at 15,090 ft (4 600 m); normal cruise, 247 mph (397 km/h); range with max. fuel and no reserves, 1,490 mls (2 400 km), with max. payload and no reserves, 650 mls (1 050 km); initial climb, 1,496 ft/min (7,6 m/sec); service ceiling, 26,250 ft (8 000 m).

Weights: Empty equipped, 15,286 lb (6 934 kg); basic operational, 15,873 lb (7 200 kg); max. take-off, 23,370 lb (10 600 kg).

Accommodation: Basic flight crew of two and standard seating for 26 passengers in three-abreast rows (two to starboard and one to port of aisle). Alternative arrangement for 29 passengers.

Status: Development aircraft for C-series of the Frégate flown in July 1968 and series production of N 262C initiated 1970 alongside military counterpart, the N 262D for the *Armée de l'Air.*

Notes: The N 262C is similar to the initial production model of the Frégate, the N 262A, apart from its more powerful engines (the earlier model having Bastan VIs) and new wing-tips improving low-speed handling. The *Armée de l'Air* has accepted six A-series Frégates and, from August 1971, received 18 D-series aircraft, and the *Aéronavale* had previously received 15 examples of the N 262A model.

AÉROSPATIALE N 262C FRÉGATE

Dimensions: Span, 71 ft 10¼ in (21,90 m); length, 63 ft 3 in (19,28 m); height, 20 ft 4 in (6,21 m); wing area, 592 sq ft (55,0 m²).

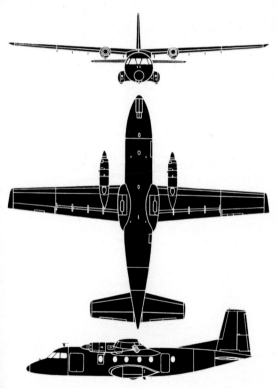

AÉROSPATIALE RALLYE 180 GT

Country of Origin: France.

Type: Light cabin monoplane.

Power Plant: One 180 hp Lycoming O-360-A3A four-cylinder horizontally-opposed engine.

Performance: Max. speed, 150 mph (240 km/h) at sea level; cruise at 75% power, 140 mph (225 km/h); normal range, 575 mls (925 km/h); initial climb rate, 787 ft/min (4,0 m/sec); service ceiling, 12,800 ft (3 900 m).

Weights: Empty equipped, 1,212 lb (550 kg); max. take-off, 2,315 lb (1 050 kg).

Accommodation: Two individual seats in front with dual controls and bench seat for two persons at the rear.

Status: The Rallye 180 GT is the 1973 production version of the MS 893 Rallye Commodore 180, first flown in prototype form on December 7, 1964, and in continuous production since 1965.

Notes: The 1973 range of Rallye light monoplanes manufactured by the Aviation Générale Division of Aérospatiale comprises, in addition to the Rallye 180 GT, the Rallye 100 (100 hp Rolls-Royce/Continental O-200-A), the Rallye 125 (125 hp Lycoming O-235-F2A), the Rallye 150 GT (150 hp Lycoming O-320-E2A), and the Rallye 220 GT (220 hp Franklin 6A-350-C1). The GT (*Grand Tourisme*) models introduce a number of changes, such as a wheel in place of control stick and a central console for engine controls, but the airframes of all versions are essentially similar. Monthly production rate at the beginning of 1973 was averaging 30.

AÉROSPATIALE RALLYE 180 GT

Dimensions: Span, 31 ft 6¼ in (9,61 m); length, 23 ft 5¾ in (7,16 m); height, 9 ft 2¼ in (2,80 m); wing area, 132 sq ft (12,30 m²).

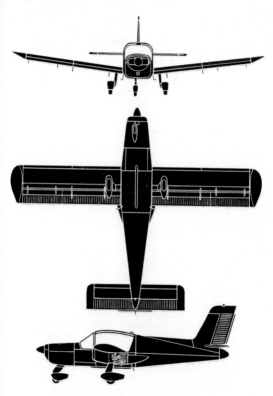

AESL CT-4 AIRTRAINER

Country of Origin: New Zealand.
Type: Side-by-side two-seat primary trainer.
Power Plant: One 210 hp Continental IO-360-D six-cylinder horizontally-opposed engine.
Performance: Max. speed, 180 mph (290 km/h) at sea level, 173 mph (278 km/h) at 5,000 ft (1 605 m); cruise at 75% power, 155 mph (250 km/h) at sea level, 149 mph (240 km/h) at 5,000 ft (1 605 m); range with 10% reserves, 808 mls (1 300 km) at 146 mph (235 km/h), 770 mls (1 240 km) at 152 mph (244 km/h); initial climb, 1,345 ft/min (6,8 m/sec).
Weights: Empty equipped, 1,520 lb (690 kg); max. take-off, 2,350 lb (1 070 kg).
Status: Prototype flown for first time on February 21, 1972, with first production deliveries (to Royal Thai Air Force) scheduled for summer 1973.
Notes: The CT-4 Airtrainer is derived from the four-seat Victa Aircruiser which was carried to the prototype test stage in Australia, the project being purchased mid-1971 by AESL (Aero Engine Services Limited). Aerodynamically the CT-4 Airtrainer is identical to the original Australian design, apart from the ailerons and elevator, but the structure and systems have been completely reworked by AESL. An initial production order for 24 examples was placed by the Royal Thai Air Force on September 22, 1972, and the Airtrainer has been selected by the RAAF as a successor to the Winjeel, current plans calling for deliveries against an order for 37 to commence in February 1974.

AESL CT-4 AIRTRAINER

Dimensions: Span, 26 ft 0 in (7,92 m); length, 23 ft 2 in (7,06 m); height, 8 ft 6 in (2,59 m); wing area, 129 sq ft (12,00 m²).

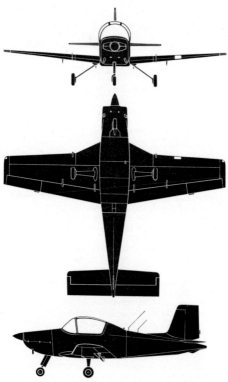

AIRBUS A300B-2

Country of Origin: International consortium.

Type: Short- to medium-range commercial transport.

Power Plant: Two 51,000 lb (23 133 kg) General Electric CF6-50C turbofans.

Performance: (Estimated) Max. cruise, 582 mph (937 km/h) at 25,000 ft (7 620 m); typical high-speed cruise, 570 mph (917 km/h) at 30,000 ft (9 145 m); typical long-range cruise, 526 mph (847 km/h) at 31,000 ft (9 450 m); range with 281 passengers, 1,615 mls (2 600 km), with max. fuel, 2,300 mls (3 700 km).

Weights: (Estimated) Typical operational empty, 186,810 lb (84 740 kg); max. take-off, 302,032 lb (137 000 kg).

Accommodation: Basic flight crew of three and basic arrangement for 281 passengers with high-density arrangement for 345 passengers.

Status: First A300B (dimensionally to B-1 standard) flown initially on October 28, 1972. Second aircraft (also to B-1 standard) was scheduled to join the test programme in February 1973, with third and fourth aircraft (to B-2 standard) commencing flight trials in June and September 1973 respectively. First delivery of A300B-2 (to Air France) scheduled for March 1974 with deliveries of longer-range A300B-4 (to Iberia and Sterling) following in 1975.

Notes: The A300B is being manufactured by an international consortium comprising Aérospatiale (France), Deutsche Airbus (Federal Germany), Hawker Siddeley (UK), CASA (Spain) and Fokker-VFW (Netherlands), the programme being managed by Airbus Industrie. The A300B-2 is the current production model, the first two aircraft being A300B-1s with a 167 ft $2\frac{1}{4}$ in (50,97 m) fuselage.

AIRBUS A300B-2

Dimensions: Span, 147 ft 1¼ in (44,84 m); length, 175 ft 11 in (53,62 m); height, 54 ft 2 in (16,53 m); wing area, 2,799 sq ft (260,0 m²).

ANTONOV AN-14M

Country of Origin: Soviet Union.

Type: Light STOL utility transport and feederliner.

Power Plant: Two 810 eshp Isotov TVD-650 turboprops.

Performance: Max. speed, 205 mph (330 km/h); max. continuous cruise, 189 mph (305 km/h); range, 560–715 mls (900–1 150 km); normal operational ceiling, 19,685 ft (6 000 m).

Weights: Empty equipped, 7,716 lb (3 500 kg); normal take-off, 12,346 lb (5 600 kg).

Accommodation: Normal flight crew of two and tip-up seats for 15 passengers in five rows of three, or six stretchers and one medical attendant for aeromedical role.

Status: Initial prototype flown September 1969 with production deliveries scheduled to commence during 1973.

Notes: Despite its designation, the An-14M possesses no more than a similarity of basic configuration with the piston-engined An-14 Pchelka, and has undergone progressive changes to wing, tail assembly and undercarriage during the course of development. The first prototype was fitted with retractable undercarriage, but this feature was discarded in favour of a fixed undercarriage at an early stage in the test programme, and the photograph above depicts a prototype with the original fin-and-rudder assembly, that of the production model being illustrated by the general arrangement drawing. The An-14M is to be used for a variety of roles, including fire-fighting, geological survey and freight transportation. In the agricultural role up to 1,764 lb (800 kg) of chemicals may be carried for spraying or dusting.

ANTONOV AN-14M

Dimensions: Span, 72 ft 2⅛ in (22,00 m); length, 42 ft 6⅞ in (12,98 m); height, 15 ft 1 in (4,60 m).

ANTONOV AN-22 ANTEI (COCK)

Country of Origin: USSR.

Type: Heavy military and commercial freighter.

Power Plant: Four 15,000 shp Kuznetsov NK-12MA turbo-props.

Performance: Max. speed, 460 mph (740 km/h); max. cruise, 422 mph (679 km/h); range with 99,208 lb (45 000 kg) payload, 6,835 mls (11 000 km) at 373 mph (600 km/h), with 176,370 lb (80 000 kg) payload, 3,107 mls (5 000 km) at 404 mph (650 km/h); cruise altitude, 26,250–32,800 ft (8 000–10 000 m).

Weights: Empty equipped, 251,327 lb (114 000 kg); max. take-off, 551,156 lb (250 000 kg).

Accommodation: Crew of five–six and cabin for 28–29 passengers between freight hold and flight deck. Freight hold can accommodate three tracked carriers for single Frog or twin Ganef surface-to-air missiles, self-propelled guns, etc.

Status: In production for both military and commercial use. First of five prototypes flown February 27, 1965, with first production deliveries following in the spring of 1967.

Notes: Capable of taking-off in fully loaded condition within 1,420 yards (1 300 m) and landing within 875 yards (800 m), the An-22 Antei (Antheus) is used extensively by the Soviet Air Forces and *Aeroflot*. The majority of An-22s now feature a reconfigured nose section (as illustrated above and on the opposite page) embodying two radars.

ANTONOV AN-22 ANTEI (COCK)

Dimensions: Span, 211 ft 3½ in (64,40 m); length, 189 ft 8 in (57,80 m); height, 41 ft 1 in (12,53 m); wing area, 3,713·55 sq ft (345 m²).

29

ANTONOV AN-26 (CURL)

Country of Origin: USSR.
Type: Short- to medium-range military and commercial freighter.
Power Plant: Two 2,820 eshp Ivchenko AI-24T turboprops and one (starboard nacelle) 1,984 lb (900 kg) Tumansky RU-19-300 auxiliary turbojet.
Performance: Max. speed, 335 mph (540 km/h) at 19,685 ft (6 000 m); normal cruise, 280 mph (450 km/h) at 19,685 ft (6 000 m); range cruise, 273 mph (440 km/h) at 22,965 ft (7 000 m); range with 3,307 lb (1 500 kg) payload and reserves, 1,553 mls (2 500 km), with 11,023 lb (5 000 kg) payload and reserves, 808 mls (1 300 km); service ceiling, 24,935 ft (7 600 m).
Weights: Empty equipped, 37,258 lb (16 914 kg); max. take-off, 52,911 lb (24 000 kg).
Accommodation: Normal crew of five with folding seats for up to 38 passengers/troops along main cabin walls. Direct rear loading for freight or vehicles and provision for air-dropping over rear ramp.
Status: Production deliveries for both military and commercial use reportedly commenced 1969.
Notes: Derivative of the commercial An-24RT intended for both military and civil applications, the An-26 differs from An-24 variants in having a completely redesigned rear fuselage of "beavertail" type, and large paradrop observation blister to port below and aft of the flight deck. Structurally, the An-26 is essentially similar to the An-24 Series II (see 1969 edition), and has an auxiliary turbojet in the starboard nacelle as introduced by the An-24RT.

ANTONOV AN-26 (CURL)

Dimensions: Span, 95 ft 10 in (29,20 m); length, 78 ft 1 in (23,80 m); height, 28 ft 1⅔ in (8,57 m); wing area, 779·95 sq ft (72,46 m²).

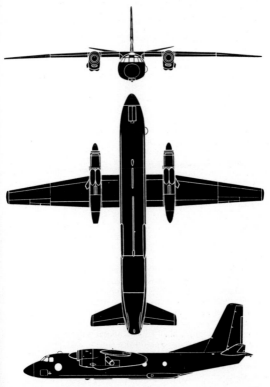

BAC ONE-ELEVEN 475

Country of Origin: United Kingdom.
Type: Short- to medium-range commercial transport.
Power Plant: Two 12,550 lb (5 692 kg) Rolls-Royce Spey 512-14-DW turbofans.
Performance: Max. cruise, 548 mph (882 km/h) at 21,000 ft (6 400 m); econ. cruise, 507 mph (815 km/h) at 25,000 ft (7 620 m); range with reserves for 230 mls (370 km) diversion and 45 min, 2,095 mls (3 370 km), with capacity payload, 1,590 mls (2 560 km); initial climb rate at 345 mph (555 km/h), 2,350 ft/min (11,93 m/sec).
Weights: Basic operational, 51,814 lb (23 502 kg); max. take-off, 92,000 lb (41 730 kg).
Accommodation: Basic flight crew of two and up to 89 passengers. Typical mixed-class arrangement provides for 16 first-class (four-abreast) and 49 tourist-class (five-abreast) passengers.
Status: Aerodynamic prototype of One-Eleven 475 flown August 27, 1970 followed by first production model on April 5, 1971, with certification and first production deliveries following in June.
Notes: The One-Eleven 475 combines the standard fuselage of the Series 400 with the redesigned wing and uprated engines of the Series 500 (see 1970 edition), coupling these with a low-pressure undercarriage to permit operation from gravel or low-strength sealed runways. The One-Eleven prototype flew on August 20, 1963, production models including the physically similar Series 200 and 300 with 10,330 lb (4 686 kg) Spey 506s and 11,400 lb (5 170 kg) Spey 511s, the Series 400 modified for US operation, and the Series 500 which is similar to the 475 apart from the fuselage and undercarriage.

BAC ONE-ELEVEN 475

Dimensions: Span, 93 ft 6 in (28,50 m); length, 93 ft 6 in (28,50 m); height, 24 ft 6 in (7,47 m); wing area, 1,031 sq ft (95,78 m²).

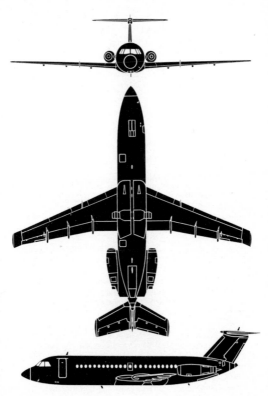

BAC 167 STRIKEMASTER

Country of Origin: United Kingdom.
Type: Side-by-side two-seat basic trainer and light attack and counter-insurgency aircraft.
Power Plant: One 3,410 lb (1 547 kg) Rolls-Royce Viper 535 turbojet.
Performance: Max. speed, 450 mph (724 km/h) at sea level, 472 mph (760 km/h) at 20,000 ft (6 096 m); range at 8,355 lb (3 789 kg), 725 mls (1 166 km), at 10,500 lb (4 762 kg), 1,238 mls (1 992 km), at 11,500 lb (5 216 kg), 1,382 mls (2 224 km); initial climb at 8,355 lb (3 789 kg), 5,250 ft/min (26,67 m/sec); time to 30,000 ft (9 150 m), 8 min 45 sec, to 40,000 ft (12 200 m), 15 min 30 sec.
Weights: Empty equipped, 5,850 lb (2 653 kg); normal take-off (pilot training), 8,355 lb (3 789 kg), (navigational training), 9,143 lb (4 147 kg); max., 11,500 lb (5 216 kg).
Armament: Provision for two 7,62-mm FN machine guns with 550 rpg and eight underwing stores stations for up to 3,000 lb (1 360 kg) of stores.
Status: Prototype Strikemaster flown October 26, 1967, with production deliveries following late 1968. Versions ordered and which differ only in equipment specified include Mk. 80 (Saudi Arabia), Mk. 81 (South Yemen), Mk. 82 (Muscat and Oman), Mk. 83 (Kuwait), Mk. 84 (Singapore), Mk. 87 (Kenya), Mk. 88 (New Zealand) and Mk. 89 (Ecuador). Total of 111 Strikemasters contracted for by beginning of 1973.
Notes: Derivative of BAC 145 (see 1971 edition) from which it differs primarily in having a more powerful engine, some local structural strengthening, and additional stores stations.

BAC 167 STRIKEMASTER

Dimensions: Span, 35 ft 4 in (10,77 m); length, 34 ft 0 in (10,36 m); height, 10 ft 2 in (3,10 m); wing area, 213·7 sq ft (19,80 m²).

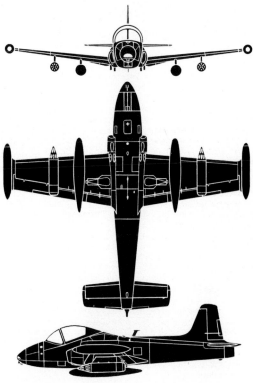

BAC-AÉROSPATIALE CONCORDE

Countries of Origin: United Kingdom and France.
Type: Long-range supersonic commercial transport.
Power Plant: Four 38,050 lb (17 259 kg) reheat Rolls-Royce/SNECMA Olympus 593 Mk. 602 turbojets.
Performance: Max. cruise, 1,450 mph (2 330 km/h) or Mach 2·2 at 54,500 ft (16 000 m); max. range cruise, 1,350 mph (2 170 km/h) or Mach 2·05; max. fuel range with FAR reserves and 17,000-lb (7 710-kg) payload, 4,400 mls (7 080 km); max. payload range, 3,600 mls (5 790 km) at 616 mph (990 km/h) or Mach 0·93 at 30,000 ft (9 100 m), 4,020 mls (6 470 km) at 1,350 mph (2 170 km/h) or Mach 2·05 at 54,500 ft (16 000 m); initial climb, 5,000 ft/min (25,4 m/sec).
Weights: Operational empty, 169,000 lb (76 650 kg); max. take-off, 385,810 lb (175 000 kg).
Accommodation: Normal flight crew of three and economy-class seating for 128 passengers. Alternative high-density arrangement for 144 passengers.
Status: First and second prototypes flown March 2 and April 9, 1969 respectively. First of two pre-production aircraft flew December 17, 1971, the second (illustrated above) flying on January 10, 1973.
Notes: Both specification and general-arrangement silhouette apply to production Concorde, the prototypes featuring a shorter fuselage and differences in cockpit visor and wing profile. The Concorde reached Mach 2·0 on November 4, 1970, the prototypes having 34,700 lb (15 740 kg) Olympus 593-3Bs, and the definitive engine for the production model will be the Olympus 612 of 39,940 lb (18 116 kg). Sixteen production Concordes were under construction by beginning of 1973 (plus long lead time items for six more).

BAC-AÉROSPATIALE CONCORDE

Dimensions: Span, 84 ft 0 in (25,60 m); length, 203 ft $8\frac{3}{4}$ in (62,10 m); height, 39 ft $10\frac{1}{4}$ in (12,15 m); wing area, 3,856 sq ft (358,25 m²).

BEECHCRAFT B99

Country of Origin: USA.

Type: Light commercial feederliner.

Power Plant: Two 680 shp Pratt & Whitney PT6A-28 turboprops.

Performance: Max. cruise, 284 mph (457 km/h) at 12,000 ft (3 650 m); econ. cruise, 279 mph (449 km/h) at 8,000 ft (2 440 m); range cruise, 216 mph (348 km/h) at 8,000 ft (2 440 m); max. fuel range, 887 mls (1 427 km) at 8,000 ft (2 440 m) with 45 min reserves at 279 mph (449 km/h), 1,048 mls (1 686 km) at 216 mph (348 km/h).

Weights: Empty equipped (standard 15-seater), 5,780 lb (2 621 kg); max. take-off, 10,900 lb (4 944 kg).

Accommodation: Normal flight crew of two and 15 passengers in individual seats on each side of central aisle. Optional 8-seat business executive transport arrangement. An 800-lb (363-kg) capacity ventral cargo pod (shown fitted above and on opposite page) may be carried.

Status: The prototype Model 99 was flown in July 1966 and the first production delivery followed on May 2, 1968, the 100th being delivered on April 28, 1969. The 36th production Model 99 served as a prototype for the Model 99A, deliveries of which began in 1969, and the 148th Model 99 series airliner delivered in November 1972 was the first to B99 standards.

Notes: Standard Model 99 has 550 shp PT6A-20 turboprops. Model B99 possesses similar power to that of Model 99A (see 1972 edition) but has a 500-lb (227-kg) increase in max. take-off weight, a new heavy-duty flap system and a new elevator system.

BEECHCRAFT B99

Dimensions: Span, 45 ft $10\frac{1}{2}$ in (14,00 m); length, 44 ft $6\frac{2}{3}$ in (13,58 m); height, 14 ft $4\frac{1}{3}$ in (4,40 m); wing area, 279·7 sq ft (25,985 m²).

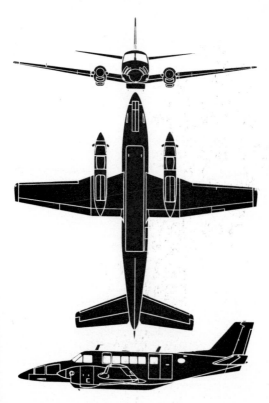

BEECHCRAFT KING AIR E90

Country of Origin: USA.

Type: Light business executive transport.

Power Plant: Two 680 shp Pratt & Whitney (UACL) PT6A-28 turboprops.

Performance: Max. cruise, 287 mph (462 km/h) at 12,000 ft (3 655 m), 285 mph (459 km/h) at 16,000 ft (4 875 m), 282 mph (454 km/h) at 21,000 ft (6 400 m); max. range, 1,704 mls (2 742 km) at 16,000 ft (4 875 m), 1,870 mls (3 009 km) at 21,000 ft (6 400 m); service ceiling, 27,620 ft (8 419 m).

Weights: Empty equipped, 5,876 lb (2 665 kg); max. take-off, 10,100 lb (4 581 kg).

Accommodation: Flight crew of two and standard arrangement of four individual seats in main cabin with optional arrangements for up to eight passengers.

Status: King Air E90 introduced May 1972, in which month first customer deliveries were made.

Notes: The King Air E90 is basically a more powerful version of the King Air C90, employing similar turboprops to those of the larger King Air A100 (see 1972 edition). Both the C90 and A100 remain in production, and at the time the E90 was added to the King Air range Beech had delivered 556 King Air 90s and 110 King Air 100s. The King Air flew for the first time on January 20, 1964, production deliveries commencing during the following October, and the type has remained continuously in production in progressively improved versions. The King Air C90 was selected in 1972 by the Japanese Maritime Self-Defence Force as the standard instrument trainer of its air component.

BEECHCRAFT KING AIR E90

Dimensions: Span, 50 ft 3 in (15,32 m); length, 35 ft 6 in (10,82 m); height, 14 ft 2½ in (4,33 m); wing area, 293·9 sq ft (27,3 m²).

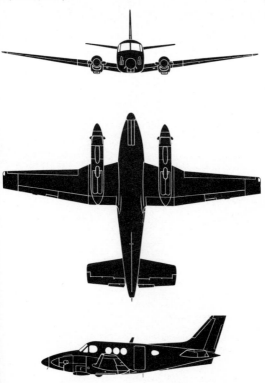

BOEING MODEL 727-200

Country of Origin: USA.

Type: Short- to medium-range commercial transport.

Power Plant: Three 14,500 lb (6 577 kg) Pratt & Whitney JT8D-9 turbofans (with 15,000 lb/6 804 kg JT8D-11s or 15,500 lb/7 030 kg JT8D-15s as options).

Performance: Max. speed, 621 mph (999 km/h) at 20,500 ft (6 250 m); max. cruise, 599 mph (964 km/h) at 24,700 ft (7 530 m); econ. cruise, 570 mph (917 km/h) at 30,000 ft (9 145 m); range with 26,400-lb (11 974-kg) payload and normal reserves, 2,850 mls (4 585 km), with max. payload (41,000 lb/18 597 kg), 1,845 mls (2 970 km); initial climb, 2,600 ft/min (13,2 m/sec); service ceiling, 33,500 ft (10 210 m).

Weights: Operational empty (basic), 97,525 lb (44 235 kg), (typical), 99,000 lb (44 905 kg); max. take-off, 190,500 lb (86 405 kg).

Accommodation: Crew of three on flight deck and six-abreast seating for 163 passengers in basic arrangement with max. seating for 189 passengers.

Status: First Model 727-100 flown February 9, 1963, with first delivery (to United) following October 29, 1963. Model 727-200 flown July 27, 1967, with first delivery (to Northeast) on December 11, 1967. Deliveries from mid-1972 have been of the so-called "Advanced 727-200" (to which specification refers) and a total of 1,010 Model 727s of all versions had been ordered by the beginning of 1973, of which 912 had been delivered.

Notes: The Model 727-200 is a "stretched" version of the 727-100 (see 1972 edition) and is now being offered with a 191,000 lb (86 633 kg) gross weight and increased fuel capacity.

BOEING MODEL 727-200

Dimensions: Span, 108 ft 0 in (32,92 m); length, 153 ft 2 in (46,69 m); height, 34 ft 0 in (10,36 m); wing area, 1,700 sq ft (157,9 m²).

BOEING MODEL 737-200C

Country of Origin: USA.

Type: Short-range commercial convertible cargo-passenger transport.

Power Plant: Two 15,500 lb (7 030 kg) Pratt & Whitney JT8D-15 turbofans.

Performance: Max. speed, 586 mph (943 km/h) at 23,500 ft (7 165 m); max. cruise, 576 mph (927 km/h) at 22,600 ft (6 890 m); econ. cruise, 525 mph (845 km/h) at 30,000 ft (9 145 m); range with max. fuel and reserves for 200-mile diversion and 45 min, 2,210 mls (3 555 km), max. payload and similar reserves, 2,370 mls (3 815 km).

Weights: Operational empty (all cargo), 59,750 lb (27 102 kg), (all passenger), 65,000 lb (29 483 kg); max. take-off, 116,000 lb (52 615 kg).

Accommodation: Normal flight crew of two and up to 119 passengers in six-abreast seating in all-passenger configuration, or up to 34,270 lb (15 544 kg) in cargo configuration.

Status: First Model 737-100 flown on April 9, 1967 (see 1967 edition), followed by first -200 on August 8, 1967. Approximately 310 Model 737s of all versions delivered by beginning of 1973 against total orders for 338.

Notes: All aircraft delivered since May 1971 have been completed to the so-called "Advanced 737-200/C/QC" standard (to which specification refers), embodying improvements in range and short-field performance. The 14,500 lb (6 575 kg) JT8D-9 engine and gross weight of 110,000 lb (49 900 kg) are available as options. Deliveries of a navigational training version of the Model 737-200 to the USAF as the T-43 will commence during 1973 against an initial order for 19 aircraft.

44

BOEING MODEL 737-200C

Dimensions: Span, 93 ft 0 in (28,35 m); length, 100 ft 0 in (30,48 m); height, 37 ft 0 in (11,28 m); wing area, 980 sq ft (91,05 m²).

BOEING MODEL 747B

Country of Origin: USA.

Type: Long-range large-capacity commercial transport.

Power Plant: Four 47,000 lb (21 320 kg) Pratt & Whitney JT9D-7W turbofans.

Performance: Max. speed at 600,000 lb (272 155 kg), 608 mph (978 km/h) at 30,000 ft (9 150 m); long-range cruise, 589 mph (948 km/h) at 35,000 ft (10 670 m); range with max. fuel and FAR reserves, 7,080 mls (11 395 km), with 79,618-lb (36 114-kg) payload, 6,620 mls (10 650 km); cruise ceiling, 45,000 ft (13 715 m).

Weights: Operational empty, 361,216 lb (163 844 kg); max. take-off, 775,000 lb (351 540 kg).

Accommodation: Normal flight crew of three and basic accommodation for 66 first-class and 308 economy-class passengers. Alternative layouts for 447 or 490 economy-class passengers in nine-abreast and 10-abreast seating respectively.

Status: First Model 747-100 flown on February 9, 1969, and first commercial services (by Pan American) inaugurated January 22, 1970. The first Model 747-200 (747B), the 88th aircraft off the assembly line, flown October 11, 1970.

Notes: Principal production versions of the Model 747 are currently the -100 and -200 series, the latter having greater fuel capacity and increased maximum take-off weight, convertible passenger/cargo and all-cargo versions of the -200 series (alias Model 747B) being designated 747C and 747F respectively. The first production example of the latter flew on November 30, 1971, and was delivered (to Lufthansa) during March 1972. The Model 747SR, a short-range version of the 747-100, was ordered by Japan Air Lines in November 1972.

46

BOEING MODEL 747B

Dimensions: Span, 195 ft 8 in (59,64 m); length, 231 ft 4 in (70,51 m); height, 63 ft 5 in (19,33 m); wing area, 5,685 sq ft (528,15 m²).

BOEING EC-137D

Country of Origin: USA.
Type: Airborne warning and control system development aircraft.
Power Plant: Four 19,000 lb (8 618 kg) Pratt & Whitney JT3D-7 turbofans.
Performance: No details have been released for publication, but max. and econ. cruise speeds are likely to be generally similar to those of the equivalent commercial Model 707-320B (i.e., 627 mph/1 010 km/h and 550 mph/886 km/h respectively).
Weights: No details available.
Accommodation: The proposed production derivative, the E-3A, will carry an operational crew of 17 which may be increased according to mission.
Status: First of two EC-137D development aircraft flown February 9, 1972. At the beginning of 1973 it was proposed that five pre-production examples of the operational derivative, the E-3A, should be built with deliveries commencing in the spring of 1975. Subsequent production of 42 E-3As is envisaged.
Notes: As part of a programme for the development of a new AWACS (Airborne Warning And Control System) aircraft for operation by the USAF from the mid 'seventies, two Boeing 707-320B transports have been modified as EC-137D test-beds. These were employed during 1972 for competitive evaluation of the competing Hughes and Westinghouse radars, the latter having been selected as winning contender. One proposed production E-3A AWACS aircraft differs from the EC-137D primarily in having eight General Electric TF34-GE-2 turbofans paired in pylon-mounted pods.

BOEING EC-137D

Dimensions: Span, 145 ft 9 in (44,42 m); length, 152 ft 11 in (46,61 m); height, 42 ft 5 in (12,93 m); wing area, 3,050 sq ft (283,4 m²).

49

BREGUET 1150 ATLANTIC

Country of Origin: France.

Type: Long-range maritime patrol aircraft.

Power Plant: Two 6,105 ehp Hispano-built Rolls-Royce Tyne R.Ty.20 Mk. 21 turboprops.

Performance: Max. speed, 409 mph (658 km/h); max. cruise, 363 mph (584 km/h) at 19,685 ft (6 000 m), 342 mph (550 km/h) at 26,250 ft (8 000 m); range cruise, 311 mph (500 km/h) at 26,250 ft (8 000 m); max. endurance cruise, 195 mph (320 km/h); loiter endurance at range of 620 mls (1 000 km), 12 hrs; max. endurance, 18 hrs; range with 10% reserves, 4,950 mls (7 970 km); max. range, 5,590 mls (9 000 km); initial climb, 2,450 ft/min (12,44 m/sec); service ceiling, 32,800 ft (10 000 m).

Weights: Empty, 52,900 lb (24 000 kg); max. take-off, 95,900 lb (43 500 kg).

Armament: Nine 400-lb (181,4-kg) Mk. 44 acoustic torpedoes or four 1,124-lb (510-kg) L4 torpedoes plus single nuclear depth charge internally, and four AS.12 missiles beneath wings.

Accommodation: Crew of 12 of which seven accommodated in central operations compartment.

Status: First of three prototypes flown October 21, 1961, and production against total orders for 87 (40 for France, 20 for Germany, 18 for Italy and nine for the Netherlands) scheduled to continue until early 1973.

Notes: Built by French-German-Belgian-Italian-Dutch consortium with final assembly in France.

BREGUET 1150 ATLANTIC

Dimensions: Span, 119 ft $1\frac{1}{4}$ in (36,30 m); length, 104 ft $1\frac{1}{2}$ in (31,75 m); height, 37 ft $1\frac{3}{4}$ in (11,33 m); wing area, 1,295·33 sq ft (120,34 m²).

BRITTEN-NORMAN BN-2A ISLANDER

Country of Origin: United Kingdom.

Type: Light utility transport.

Power Plant: Two 260 hp Lycoming O-540-E4C5 six-cylinder horizontally-opposed engines.

Performance: Max. speed, 170 mph (273 km/h) at sea level; cruise at 75% power, 160 mph (257 km/h) at 7,000 ft (2 140 m), at 67% power, 158 mph (253 km/h) at 9,000 ft (2 750 m), at 59% power, 154 mph (248 km/h) at 13,000 ft (3 960 m); range with standard fuel, 717 mls (1 154 km) at 160 mph (257 km/h), 870 mls (1 400 km) at 154 mph (248 km/h), tip tanks, 1,040 mls (1 674 km) at 160 mph (257 km/h), 1,263 mls (2 035 km) at 154 mph (248 km/h).

Weights: Empty equipped, 3,675 lb (1 667 kg); max. take-off, 6,600 lb (2 993 kg).

Accommodation: Flight crew of one or two and up to 10 passengers on pairs of bench-type seats, or two casualty stretchers and two medical attendants for ambulance role.

Status: Prototype flown June 12, 1965, followed by first production aircraft on August 20, 1966. More than 400 ordered by beginning of 1973. Production being transferred to Fairey SA in Belgium during 1973, and 215 airframes being manufactured under contract by IRMA in Rumania.

Notes: The BN-2A-8S illustrated above and on opposite page, and to which the above specification applies, is the latest development in the Islander series, and was first flown on August 22, 1972. It features a 45·5-in (1,15-m) longer nose to provide increased baggage space, an additional cabin window each side at the rear, and provision for an additional seat row. These changes, indicated by the suffix "S" (for Stretched), are being offered as customer options.

BRITTEN-NORMAN BN-2A ISLANDER

Dimensions: Span, 49 ft 0 in (14,94 m); length, 39 ft $5\frac{1}{4}$ in (12,02 m); height, 13 ft 8 in (4,16 m); wing area, 325 sq ft (30,2 m²).

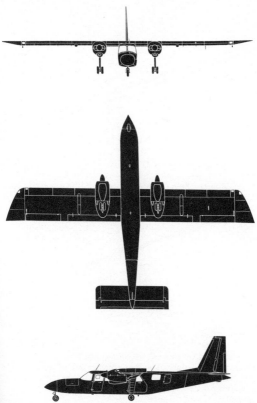

BRITTEN-NORMAN BN-2A MK III
TRISLANDER

Country of Origin: United Kingdom.

Type: Light utility transport and feederliner.

Power Plant: Three 260 hp Lycoming O-540-E4C5 six-cylinder horizontally-opposed engines.

Performance: Max. speed, 187 mph (301 km/h) at sea level; cruise at 75% power, 180 mph (290 km/h) at 6,500 ft (1 980 m), at 67% power, 175 mph (282 km/h) at 9,000 ft (2 750 m); range with max. payload, 160 mls (257 km) at 170 mph (274 km/h), with 2,400-lb (1 089-kg) payload, 700 mls (1 127 km) at 175 mph (282 km/h).

Weights: Empty equipped, 5,638 lb (2 557 kg); max. take-off, 9,350 lb (4 240 kg).

Accommodation: Flight crew of one or two, and 16—17 passengers in pairs on bench-type seats.

Status: Prototype flown September 11, 1970, with production prototype flying on March 6, 1971. First production Trislander flown April 29, 1971, and first delivery (to Aurigny) following on June 29, 1971. Trislander production was being transferred to Fairey SA late in 1972.

Notes: The Trislander is a derivative of the Islander (see pages 52—53) with which it has 75% commonality. The wingtip auxiliary fuel tanks optional on the Islander have been standardised for the Trislander.

54

BRITTEN-NORMAN BN-2A MK III TRISLANDER

Dimensions: Span, 53 ft 0 in (16,15 m); length, 43 ft 9 in (13,33 m); height, 13 ft 5¼ in (4,11 m); wing area, 337 sq ft (31,25 m²).

CASA C.212 AVIOCAR

Country of Origin: Spain.

Type: STOL utility transport, navigational trainer and photographic survey aircraft.

Power Plant: Two 776 eshp (715 shp) Garrett-AiResearch TPE 331-5-251C turboprops.

Performance: (At 13,889 lb/6 300 kg) Max. cruise, 243 mph (391 km/h) at 12,000 ft (3 658 m), 238 mph (383 km/h) at 5,000 ft (1 524 m); initial climb, 1,724 ft/min (8,76 m/sec); service ceiling, 24,605 ft (7 500 m); range with max. payload and reserves (30 min hold at 5,000 ft/ 1 524 m plus 5% take-off weight), 205 mls (330 km) at 12,500 ft (3 810 m), with max. fuel and similar reserves, 1,197 mls (1 927 km).

Weights: Empty equipped, 8,045 lb (3 650 kg); max. take-off, 13,889 lb (6 300 kg); max. payload, 4,409 lb (2 000 kg).

Accommodation: Flight crew of two and 18 passengers in commercial configuration. Ten casualty stretchers and three sitting casualties or medical attendants in ambulance configuration. Provision for up to 15 paratroops and jumpmaster or 4,409 lb (2 000 kg) of cargo.

Status: Two prototypes flown March 26 and October 23, 1971, with first of 12 pre-production examples following November 17, 1972. Initial production batch of 32 for Spanish Air Force with deliveries commencing early 1974.

Notes: To be adopted as standard utility cargo and paratroop transport by Spanish Air Force as successor to CASA-built Junkers Ju 52/3m. Of pre-production series, eight will be delivered to Air Force (six for photographic survey and two as navigational trainers), and of initial production batch 29 will be cargo-paratroop transports and three will be navigational trainers.

CASA C.212 AVIOCAR

Dimensions: Span, 62 ft 4 in (19,00 m); length, 49 ft $10\frac{1}{2}$ in (15,20 m); height, 20 ft $8\frac{3}{4}$ in (6,32 m); wing area, 430·556 sq ft (40,0 m²).

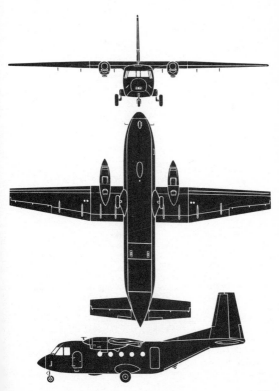

CESSNA T337G
PRESSURISED SKYMASTER

Country of Origin: USA.

Type: Light cabin monoplane.

Power Plant: Two 225 hp Teledyne Continental TSIO-360-C six-cylinder horizontally-opposed engines.

Performance: Max. speed, 250 mph (402 km/h) at 20,000 ft (6 096 m); cruise at 75% power, 228 mph (367 km/h) at 16,000 ft (4 877 m), at 65% power, 221 mph (356 km/h) at 20,000 ft (6 096 m); max. range, 1,325 mls (2 132 km) at 20,000 ft (6 096 m), 1,505 mls (2 422 km) at 16,000 ft (4 877 m); initial climb, 1,250 ft/min (6,3 m/sec).

Weights: Empty equipped, 2,900 lb (1 315 kg); max. take-off, 4,700 lb (2 132 kg).

Accommodation: Pilot and co-pilot or passenger seated side-by-side with dual controls and rear seat for two or three passengers.

Status: Derived from the non-pressurised Model 337 Skymaster, the T337G was first flown in 1971, customer deliveries commencing August 1972.

Notes: The T337G differs from earlier production models of the Skymaster in introducing a pressure shell between the two engine firewalls and a revised cabin window arrangement. It replaces the non-pressurised T337F Turbo Super Skymaster in the Cessna range. The Model 337 was introduced in February 1965, and some 1,500 aircraft of this basic type had been delivered by the beginning of 1973, plus 510 examples of two military versions, the O-2A equipped for the forward air control mission and the O-2B equipped for psychological warfare missions.

CESSNA T337G PRESSURISED SKYMASTER

Dimensions: Span, 38 ft 2 in (11,63 m); length, 29 ft 9 in (9,07 m); height, 9 ft 4 in (2,84 m); wing area, 202·5 sq ft (18,81 m²).

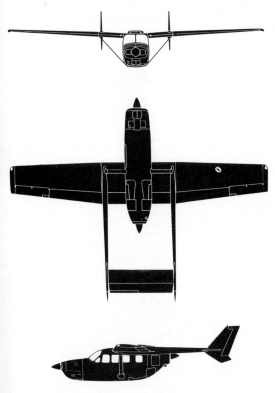

CESSNA MODEL 340

Country of Origin: USA.
Type: Light business executive transport.
Power Plant: Two 285 hp Teledyne Continental TSIO-520-K six-cylinder horizontally-opposed engines.
Performance: Max. speed, 221 mph (356 km/h) at sea level, 260 mph (418 km/h) at 16,000 ft (4 877 m); max. cruise, 219 mph (352 km/h) at 10,000 ft (3 048 m), 241 mph (388 km/h) at 20,000 ft (6 096 m); range (no reserves), 663 mls (1 067 km) at 215 mph (346 km/h) at 10,000 ft (3 048 m), 726 mls (1 168 km) at 20,000 ft (6 096 m) at 236 mph (380 km/h), (max. auxiliary fuel), 1,475 mls (2 373 km) at 20,000 ft (6 096 m); initial climb, 1,500 ft/min (7,62 m/sec); service ceiling, 26,500 ft (8 077 m).
Weights: Empty equipped, 3,723 lb (1 689 kg); max. take-off, 5,975 lb (2 710 kg).
Accommodation: Standard seating for pilot and co-pilot forward with individual seats for four passengers.
Status: Development of the Model 340 was initiated in 1969, but the first prototype was lost in the spring of 1970. Production deliveries commenced early 1972.
Notes: The first pressurised aircraft in the light-twin category at the time of its introduction, the Model 340 was evolved from the non-pressurised Model 310, introducing a new pressurised capsule-type fuselage of fail-safe design, and wings and undercarriage generally similar to those of the larger and more powerful Model 414.

CESSNA MODEL 340

Dimensions: Span, 38 ft 1⅓ in (11,62 m); length, 34 ft 4 in (10,46 m); height, 12 ft 6⅔ in (3,83 m); wing area, 184·7 sq ft (17,16 m²).

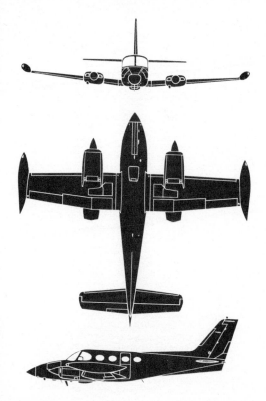

CESSNA MODEL 500 CITATION

Country of Origin: USA.

Type: Light business executive transport.

Power Plant: Two 2,200 lb (1 000 kg) Pratt & Whitney JT15D-1 turbofans.

Performance: Max. speed, 402 mph (647 km/h) at 26,400 ft (8 046 m); max. cruise, 400 mph (644 km/h) at 25,400 ft (7 740 m); range with eight persons and 45 min reserves at 90% cruise thrust, 1,397 mls (2 248 km), with two persons and same reserves at 90% cruise thrust, 1,502 mls (2 417 km); initial climb, 3,350 ft/min (17 m/sec); service ceiling, 38,400 ft (11 704 m).

Weights: Empty (excluding avionics), 5,408 lb (2 453 kg); max. take-off, 10,850 lb (4 921 kg).

Accommodation: Crew of two on separate flight deck and alternative arrangements for five or six passengers in main cabin.

Status: First of two prototypes flown on September 15, 1969, and first production Citation flown in May 1971. Customer deliveries began in October 1971 with 52 delivered by beginning of 1973 when production was five per month, an increase to 10 per month being scheduled by year's end.

Notes: The Citation places emphasis on short-field performance, balanced field length being 2,950 ft (899 m) and take-off distance to clear a 35-ft (10,7-m) obstacle being 2,300 ft (701 m), enabling the aircraft to use some 2,300 US airfields. A new gross weight of 11,650 lb (5 285 kg) is being introduced with the 71st production Citation.

CESSNA MODEL 500 CITATION

Dimensions: Span, 43 ft 8½ in (13,32 m); length, 43 ft 6 in (13,26 m); height, 14 ft 3¾ in (4,36 m); wing area, 260 sq ft (24,15 m²).

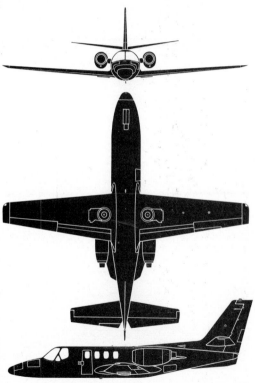

DASSAULT-BREGUET FALCON 10

Country of Origin: France.
Type: Light business executive transport.
Power Plant: Two 3,230 lb (1 465 kg) Garrett-AiResearch TFE-731-2 turbofans.
Performance: Max. cruise, 572 mph (920 km/h) at 30,000 ft (9 145 m), 495 mph (796 km/h) or Mach 0·75 at 45,000 ft (13 716 m); range with four passengers and 45 min reserves, 2,475 mls (3 980 km) at 45,000 ft (13 716 m), 1,495 mls (2 405 km) at max. cruise at 30,000 ft (9 145 m).
Weights: Empty equipped, 10,141 lb (4 600 kg); max. take-off, 18,298 lb (8 300 kg).
Accommodation: Flight crew of two with provision for third crew member on jump seat. Executive version for four passengers with alternative arrangements for eight passengers (Falcon 10A) or 10 passengers (Falcon B).
Status: First of two prototypes flown December 1, 1970, followed by second on October 15, 1971, with first production model flying on October 14, 1972. Deliveries of production aircraft scheduled for third quarter of 1973.
Notes: The Falcon 10 (also known as the Mystère 10) is basically a scaled-down version of the Falcon 20, and at a later stage in development it is proposed to offer the 2,980 lb (1 350 kg) Turboméca-SNECMA Larzac turbofan as an alternative power plant. The Falcon 10 is being offered to the *Armée de l'Air* as a military crew trainer and liaison aircraft, and two examples have been ordered for test and evaluation purposes.

DASSAULT-BREGUET FALCON 10

Dimensions: 42 ft 11 in (13,08 m); length, 44 ft 7½ in (13,60 m); height, 14 ft 5⅔ in (4,41 m); wing area, 259·4 sq ft (24,1 m²).

DASSAULT-BREGUET FALCON 20

Country of Origin: France.

Type: Light business executive transport.

Power Plant: Two 4,315 lb (1 983 kg) General Electric CF700-2D-2 turbofans.

Performance: Max. speed, 404 mph (650 km/h) at sea level, 449 mph (722 km/h) at 22,965 ft (7 000 m); max. cruise at 20,000 lb (9 072 kg), 535 mph (860 km/h) at 25,000 ft (7 620 m); econ. cruise, 466 mph (750 km/h) at 40,000 ft (12 190 m); range with eight passengers and 45 min reserves, 2,300 mls (3 580 km) at 39,370 ft (12 000 m); max. operating altitude, 42,650 ft (13 000 m).

Weights: Empty equipped, 15,972 lb (7 245 kg); max. take-off, 28,660 lb (13 000 kg).

Accommodation: Normal flight crew of two and standard arrangement for eight passengers in individual seats. Alternative arrangements available for from 10 to 14 passengers.

Status: First Falcon 20 (also known as the Mystère 20) flown May 4, 1963, followed by first production aircraft on January 1, 1965. Current production models are the Series E and Series F, these being similar apart from wing high-lift devices.

Notes: In continuous production for nine years, the Falcon 20 in its Series E and F versions differs from the Series D which they have supplanted in having slight increases in fuel capacity and range, improved electrical systems and a higher take-off weight. The Series F differs from the Series E in having a leading-edge slat inboard of each wing fence, a slotted leading-edge slat outboard of each fence, and slightly modified trailing-edge flaps. A military systems training version is known as the Falcon ST.

DASSAULT-BREGUET FALCON 20

Dimensions: Span, 53 ft 6 in (16,30 m); length, 56 ft 3 in (17,15 m); height, 17 ft 5 in (5,32 m); wing area, 440 sq ft (41,0 m²).

DASSAULT-BREGUET FALCON 30

Country of Origin: France.

Type: Commuter transport.

Power Plant: Two 5,500 lb (2 500 kg) Avco-Lycoming ALF-502D turbofans.

Performance: (Estimated) Max. cruise, 516 mph (830 km/h) at 25,000 ft (7 620 m); range cruise, 465 mph (748 km/h) at 35,000 ft (10 670 m); range (29 passengers and commuter reserves), 1,075 mls (1 730 km), (maximum payload), 652 mls (1 050 km), (max. fuel and 15 passengers), 1,740 mls (2 800 km).

Weights: Empty equipped, 19,687 lb (8 930 kg); max. take-off, 32,408 lb (14 700 kg).

Accommodation: Normal flight crew of two and alternative arrangements for 29 or 32 passengers in three-abreast seating or 38 passengers in four-abreast seating. Executive layout for 8–15 passengers.

Status: First of two prototypes scheduled to fly with small diameter fuselage (see notes) early 1973, with second prototype featuring enlarged fuselage joining the test programme during the course of the year.

Notes: The Falcon 30 (also known as the Mystère 30) is essentially a scaled-up, more powerful development of the Falcon 20 (Mystère 20), and has been evolved via an earlier project (provisionally known as the Falcon 20-T) which was to have featured a smaller-diameter fuselage capable of accommodating up to 29 passengers. Construction of a prototype had begun prior to the decision to adopt the larger-diameter fuselage, and the smaller fuselage has been retained for the first Falcon 30 prototype.

DASSAULT-BREGUET FALCON 30

Dimensions: Span, 59 ft 1½ in (18,03 m); length, 63 ft 11 in
(19,49 m); height, 19 ft 8½ in (6,01 m); wing area, 530 sq ft
(49,0 m²).

DASSAULT-BREGUET MERCURE 100

Country of Origin: France.

Type: Short-range commercial transport.

Power Plant: Two 15,500 lb (7 030 kg) Pratt & Whitney JT8D-15 turbofans.

Performance: Max. cruise, 587 mph (944 km/h) at 20,000 ft (6 100 m); econ. cruise, 575 mph (925 km/h) at 25,000 ft (7 620 m); range cruise, 512 mph (825 km/h) at 35,100 ft (10 700 m); range with max. payload (35,274 lb/16 000 kg), 466 mls (750 km) at max. cruise at 25,000 ft (7 620 m), with max. fuel and 28,420-lb (12 790-kg) payload, 1,025 mls (1 650 km); max. sea level climb at 100,000 lb (45 359 kg), 3,300 ft/min (16,76 m/sec).

Weights: Operational empty, 64,375 lb (29 200 kg); max. take-off, 116,400 lb (52 800 kg).

Accommodation: Normal flight crew of two and typical mixed-class accommodation for 132 passengers (12 first-class passengers in four-abreast seating and 120 tourist-class passengers in six-abreast seating), or alternative single-class arrangements for 140 and 150 passengers in six-abreast seating throughout.

Status: Two prototypes flown May 28, 1971, and September 7, 1972, respectively, with first production aircraft scheduled to join the test programme during the first quarter of 1973 with delivery (to Air Inter) on October 30, 1973.

Notes: The production Mercure, 2·75 ft (84 cm) longer than the prototype aircraft, is expected to receive certification in May 1973, and is being manufactured in co-operation with Aeritalia (Italy), CASA (Spain), SABCA (Belgium), F+W (Switzerland) and Canadair (Canada), all of which have contributed towards the launching programme.

DASSAULT-BREGUET MERCURE 100

Dimensions: Span, 100 ft 3 in (30,55 m); length, 114 ft 3$\frac{2}{3}$ in (34,84 m); height, 37 ft 3$\frac{1}{4}$ in (11,36 m); wing area, 1,248·6 sq ft (116,0 m²).

DASSAULT-BREGUET MIRAGE 5

Country of Origin: France.
Type: Single-seat ground attack fighter.
Power Plant: One 9,436 lb (4 280 kg) dry and 13,670 lb (6 200 kg) reheat SNECMA Atar 9C turbojet.
Performance: Max. speed (clean), 835 mph (1 335 km/h) or Mach 1·1 at sea level, 1,386 mph (2 230 km/h) or Mach 2·1 at 39,370 ft (12 000 m); cruise, 594 mph (956 km/h) at 36,090 ft (11 000 m); combat radius with 2,000-lb (907-kg) bomb load (hi-lo-hi profile), 805 mls (1 300 km), (lo-lo-lo profile), 400 mls (650 km); time to 36,090 ft (11 000 m) at Mach 0·9, 3 min, to 49,210 ft (15 000 m) at Mach 1·8, 6 min 50 sec.
Weights: Empty equipped, 14,550 lb (6 600 kg); max. loaded, 29,760 lb (13 500 kg).
Armament: Two 30-mm DEFA 5-52 cannon with 125 rpg and seven external ordnance stations. Maximum external load (ordnance and fuel), 9,260 lb (4 200 kg).
Status: Prototype flown May 19, 1967, and first deliveries (to Peru) following May 1968. Assembly (for Belgian Air Force) completed in Belgium by SABCA late 1972.
Notes: The Mirage 5 is an export version of the Mirage IIIE (see 1967 edition) optimised for the ground attack role and featuring simplified avionics. Orders at beginning of 1973 included 28 for Pakistan, 16 for Peru (including two two-seaters), 14 for Colombia (plus four two-seat Mirage IIIs), 106 for Belgium (including 16 two-seaters and 63 for tac-recce role), 110 for Libya (including 10 two-seaters), 14 for Abu Dhabi, and 50 for the *Armée de l'Air*.

72

DASSAULT-BREGUET MIRAGE 5

Dimensions: Span, 26 ft 11½ in (8,22 m); length, 51 ft 0¼ in (15,55 m); height, 13 ft 11½ in (4,25 m); wing area, 375·12 sq ft (34,85 m²).

DASSAULT-BREGUET MIRAGE F1

Country of Origin: France.
Type: Single-seat multi-purpose fighter.
Power Plant: One 11,023 lb (5 000 kg) dry and 15,873 lb (7 200 kg) reheat SNECMA Atar 9K-50 turbojet.
Performance: Max. speed (clean), 915 mph (1 472 km/h) or Mach 1·2 at sea level, 1,450 mph (2 335 km/h) or Mach 2·2 at 39,370 ft (12 000 m); range cruise, 550 mph (885 km/h) at 29,530 ft (9 000 m); range with max. external fuel, 2,050 mls (3 300 km), with max. external combat load of 8,818 lb (4 000 kg), 560 mls (900 km), with external combat load of 4,410 lb (2 000 kg), 1,430 mls (2 300 km); service ceiling, 65,600 ft (20 000 m).
Weights: Empty, 16,314 lb (7 400 kg); loaded (clean), 24,030 lb (10 900 kg); max. take-off, 32,850 lb (14 900 kg).
Armament: Two 30-mm DEFA cannon and (intercept) 1-3 Matra 530 and two AIM-9 Sidewinder AAMs, or (attack) eight 882-lb (400-kg) bombs, six 66 imp gal (300 l) napalm tanks, five 18-rocket pods, or mix of bombs and missiles, the latter including the AS.30 and AS.37 Martel ASMs.
Status: First of four prototypes flown December 23, 1966. Eighty-five ordered for *Armée de l'Air* by beginning of 1973 with deliveries scheduled to commence in July 1973. Licence manufacture is to be undertaken in South Africa.
Notes: Initial model for *Armée de l'Air* intended primarily for high-altitude intercept role. Proposed versions include F1A for day ground attack role, the F1B two-seat trainer, the F1C interceptor, the F1E multi-role version, and the F1R reconnaissance model. Later models may receive the SNECMA M53 turbojet with a reheat thrust of approximately 18,740 lb (8 500 kg). Fifteen Mirage F1s have been ordered by Spain.

DASSAULT-BREGUET MIRAGE F1

Dimensions: Span, 27 ft $6\frac{3}{4}$ in (8,40 m); length, 49 ft $2\frac{1}{2}$ in (15,00 m); height, 14 ft 9 in (4,50 m); wing area, 269·098 sq ft (25 m²).

DASSAULT-BREGUET MIRAGE G8

Country of Origin: France.

Type: Experimental multi-purpose fighter.

Power Plant: Two 15,873 lb (7 200 kg) reheat SNECMA Atar 9K-50 turbojets.

Performance: (Estimated) Max. speed, 990 mph (1 590 km/h) or Mach 1·3 at sea level, 1,650 mph (2 655 km/h) or Mach 2·5 at 41,000 ft (12 500 m).

Weights: Approx. max. take-off, 51,367 lb (23 300 kg).

Status: First Mirage G8 prototype flown on May 8, 1971, with second following on July 13, 1972.

Notes: The Mirage G8 has been derived from the single-engined Mirage G1 (see 1971 edition) and is intended to provide a basis for an advanced combat aircraft for introduction by the *Armée de l'Air* towards the latter part of the present decade. The first prototype, the Mirage G8-01, is a two-seater which has served primarily for investigation of the flight envelope, and the second prototype, the Mirage G8-02, is a single-seater intended primarily for weapon system development. Wing sweep can be varied between 23 deg in the furthest forward position and 73 deg in the furthest aft position, but consideration is being given to development of a variant of the basic design with a fixed-geometry wing swept 55 deg. It is possible that one of the Mirage G8 prototypes will be re-engined with Snecma M53 engines of 18,650 lb (8 460 kg) thrust with reheat, as these are to be specified by the *Armée de l'Air* for its future fighter, the specification for which remained fluid in other respects at the time of closing for press.

DASSAULT-BREGUET MIRAGE G8

Dimensions: *No details available for publication at the time of closing for press.*

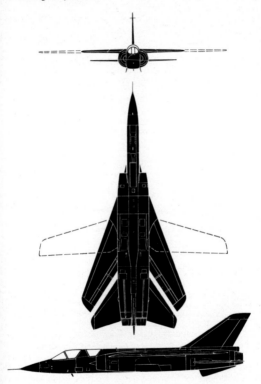

DASSAULT-BREGUET/DORNIER
ALPHA JET

Countries of Origin: France and Federal Germany.

Type: Two-seat light tactical aircraft and advanced trainer.

Power Plant: Two 2,960 lb (1 345 kg) SNECMA/Turbo-méca Larzac 04 turbofans.

Performance: (Estimated) Max. speed (clean), 633 mph (1 020 km/h) at sea level, 580 mph (933 km/h) at 36,090 ft (11 000 m); max. range (with external fuel), 1,243 mls (2 000 km) at 485 mph (780 km/h); max. endurance, 2 hr 35 min; typical endurance (low-level training mission without external fuel), 1 hr 40 min; service ceiling, 45,930 ft (14 000 m).

Weights: Empty equipped, 6,945–7,275 lb (3 150–3 300 kg); normal loaded (trainer), 9,744 lb (4 420 kg); max. take-off (trainer), 10,542 lb (4 782 kg), (strike), 15,430 lb (7 000 kg).

Armament: (Strike) One 30-mm DEFA cannon with 150 rounds beneath fuselage and four underwing stores stations each capable of carrying one 250-lb (113,4-kg), 500-lb (226,8-kg) or 1,000-lb (453,6-kg) bomb, a 600-lb (272-kg) cluster dispenser or a pod containing 36 2·75-in (7-cm) rockets.

Status: First of four prototypes to fly at Toulouse at the end of 1973 with the remaining three following during the course of 1974, the second and fourth flying at Munich. Planned production of some 400 for *Armée de l'Air* and *Luftwaffe* with deliveries commencing 1976 from two final assembly lines (Toulouse and Munich).

Notes: Alpha Jet to be used for basic and advanced training by the *Armée de l'Air* and for ground attack by the *Luftwaffe*.

DASSAULT-BREGUET/DORNIER ALPHA JET

Dimensions: Span, 30 ft 0½ in (9,16 m); length, 39 ft 6¾ in (12,05 m); height, 12 ft 8 in (3,86 m); wing area, 188·4 sq ft (17,5 m²).

DE HAVILLAND CANADA DHC-6
TWIN OTTER SERIES 300

Country of Origin: Canada.

Type: STOL utility transport and feederliner.

Power Plant: Two 652 eshp Pratt & Whitney PT6A-27 turboprops.

Performance: Max. cruise, 210 mph (338 km/h) at 10,000 ft (3 050 m); range at max. cruise with 3,250-lb (1 474-kg) payload, 745 mls (1 198 km), with 14 passengers and 45 min reserves, 780 mls (1 255 km); initial climb at 12,500 lb (5 670 kg), 1,600 ft/min (8,1 m/sec); service ceiling, 26,700 ft (8 138 m).

Weights: Basic operational (including pilot), 7,000 lb (3 180 kg); max. take-off, 12,500 lb (5 670 kg).

Accommodation: Flight crew of one or two and accommodation for up to 20 passengers in basic commuter arrangement. Optional commuter layouts for 18 or 19 passengers, and 13–20-passenger utility version.

Status: First of five (Series 100) pre-production aircraft flown May 20, 1965. Series 100 superseded by Series 200 (see 1969 edition) in April 1968, the latter being joined by the Series 300 with the 231st aircraft off the assembly line, deliveries of this version commencing spring 1969. Total of 359 ordered by beginning of 1973 when production was continuing at five per month.

Notes: Series 100 and 200 Twin Otters feature a shorter nose and have 579 eshp PT6A-20s, and the Twin Otter is available as a floatplane. The Twin Otter serves with the Canadian armed forces in the SAR and utility roles as the CC-138.

DHC-6 TWIN OTTER SERIES 300

Dimensions: Span, 65 ft 0 in (19,81 m); length, 51 ft 9 in (15,77 m); height, 18 ft 7 in (5,66 m); wing area, 420 sq ft (39,02 m²).

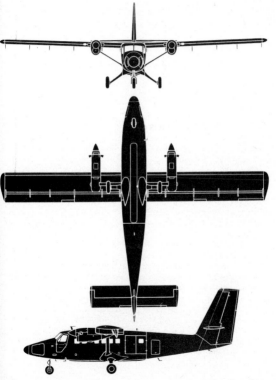

DORNIER DO 28D-2 SKYSERVANT

Country of Origin: Federal Germany.

Type: Light STOL utility aircraft.

Power Plant: Two 380 hp Lycoming IGSO-540-A1E six-cylinder horizontally-opposed engines.

Performance: Max. speed, 199 mph (320 km/h) at 10,000 ft (3 050 m); max. cruise at 75% power, 178 mph (286 km/h) at 10,000 ft (3 050 m); econ. cruise, 143 mph (230 km/h); range with max. fuel and without reserves at econ. cruise, 1,143 mls (1 837 km); initial climb, 1,180 ft/min (6 m/sec); service ceiling, 24,280 ft (7 400 m).

Weights: Empty, 4,775 lb (2 166 kg); max. take-off, 8,050 lb (3 650 kg).

Accommodation: Flight crew of one or two, and 12 passengers in individual seats in main cabin, 13 passengers in inward-facing folding seats, or (ambulance role) five casualty stretchers and five seats for medical attendants or sitting casualties.

Status: First of three prototype Do 28Ds flown February 23, 1966, with production deliveries commencing summer 1967. Total of 100 Do 28Ds delivered against orders for nearly 200 by October 1972, and production rate of six–eight per month at beginning of 1973.

Notes: Total of 125 Do 28Ds in process of delivery to *Luftwaffe* (105) and *Marineflieger* (20), four of those for the former service are used by the VIP transport unit, the *Flugbereitschaft*. The 50th Skyservant for the German armed forces was handed over in October 1972. The Skyservant may be fitted with wheel-ski gear or floats.

DORNIER DO 28D-2 SKYSERVANT

Dimensions: Span, 50 ft 10¾ in (15,50 m); length, 37 ft 4¾ in (11,40 m); height, 12 ft 9½ in (3,90 m); wing area, 308 sq ft (28,6 m²).

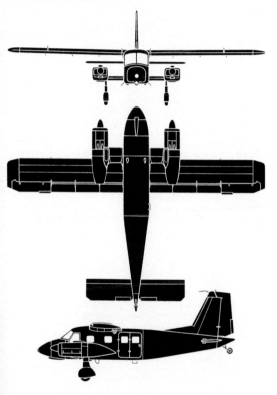

EMBRAER EMB-110 BANDEIRANTE

Country of Origin: Brazil.
Type: Light general-purpose and utility aircraft.
Power Plant: Two 680 shp Pratt & Whitney (UACL) PT6A-27 turboprops.
Performance: Max. cruise, 260 mph (418 km/h) at 9,840 ft (3 000 m); max. range (with 30 min reserves), 1,150 mls (1 850 km); initial climb, 1,968 ft/min (10 m/sec); service ceiling (at 10,692 lb/4 850 kg), 27,950 ft (8 520 m).
Weights: Empty equipped, 6,437 lb (2 920 kg); max. take-off, 11,243 lb (5 100 kg).
Accommodation: Pilot and co-pilot side-by-side on flight deck with full dual controls. Standard cabin arrangement provides six individual seats on each side of central aisle. Accommodation for four stretcher patients and two medical attendants in the aeromedical role.
Status: First of three prototypes flown October 26, 1968, with second and third following on October 19, 1969, and June 25, 1970, respectively. The first pre-series aircraft flew on August 15, 1972, and production tempo scheduled to attain four per month by the end of 1973 against an order for 80 aircraft from the *Fôrça Aérea Brasileira.*
Notes: Being manufactured by EMBRAER (Emprêsa Brasileira de Aeronáutica SA), the Bandeirante is intended to fulfil light transport, liaison, aeromedical and navigational tasks in the *Fôrça Aérea Brasileira.* Commercial variants of the Bandeirante are foreseen and a pressurised version, the EMB-120, is currently under development.

EMBRAER EMB-110 BANDEIRANTE

Dimensions: Span, 50 ft 2¼ in (15,30 m); length, 46 ft 8½ in (14,22 m); height, 15 ft 6 in (4,73 m); wing area, 312·13 sq ft (29,00 m²).

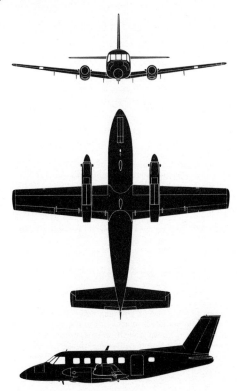

FAIRCHILD A-10A

Country of Origin: USA.
Type: Single-seat close-support aircraft.
Power Plant: Two 9,275 lb (4 207 kg) General Electric TF34-GE-2 turbofans.
Performance: Max. speed (estimated) at 25,500 lb (11 567 kg), 500 mph (805 km/h) at sea level; approx. mission radius (with 9,500 lb/4 309 kg useful payload and including 2 hrs loiter), 300 mls (480 km).
Weights: Approx. operational empty, 21,300 lb (9 661 kg); approx. max. take-off, 45,825 lb (20 786 kg).
Armament: One 20-mm M-61 rotary cannon (to be replaced by 30-mm GAU-8/A cannon in proposed production model) and up to 18,500 lb (8 392 kg) of ordnance on 11 external pylons. Typical possible loads include 24 Mk. 82 500-lb (227-kg) bombs, 16 M-117 750-lb (340-kg) bombs, four Mk. 84 2,000-lb (907-kg) bombs, 20 Rockeye 11 cluster bombs, or nine AGM-65 Maverick missiles.
Status: First of two prototypes flown May 10, 1972, followed by second on July 21, 1972. An initial batch of 10 is scheduled for delivery from late 1974.
Notes: Designed to meet the USAF's A-X close-support aircraft requirement, the A-10A participated in a fly-off contest with the Northrop A-9A (see 1972 edition) during the closing months of 1972 at which time eventual orders for up to 600 of the selected aircraft were anticipated. The A-10A was announced winning contender on January 18, 1973. The unusual positioning of the turbofans has been selected to reduce vulnerability to foreign object ingestion when operating from short battlefield-area airstrips.

FAIRCHILD A-10A

Dimensions: Span, 55 ft 0 in (16,76 m); length, 52 ft 7 in (16,03 m); height, 14 ft 5½ in (4,41 m); wing area, 488 sq ft (45,13 m²).

FAIRCHILD AU-23A PEACEMAKER

Country of Origin: USA.

Type: Light counter-insurgency and utility aircraft.

Power Plant: One 665 shp Garrett-AiResearch TPE 331-1-101F turboprop.

Performance: Max. cruise, 164 mph (264 km/h) at 10,000 ft (3 050 m); econ. cruise, 144 mph (231 km/h) at 10,000 ft (3 050 m); max. range (with two 42 Imp gal/190 l underwing tanks), 1,044 mls (1 680 km); initial climb, 1,610 ft/min (8,12 m/sec); service ceiling, 27,875 ft (8 500 m).

Weights: Empty equipped, 2,612 lb (1 185 kg); normal take-off, 4,850 lb (2 200 kg); max. overload, 6,000 lb (2 722 kg).

Armament: One side-firing flexibly-mounted 20-mm XM-197 cannon or two side-firing MXU-470 Miniguns plus ordnance on one under-fuselage and four underwing hardpoints.

Accommodation: Pilot seated to port with passenger to starboard. Freight or 6–10 passengers may be carried.

Status: Two prototype AU-23As followed in 1972 by evaluation batch of 15 aircraft.

Notes: The AU-23A (version of the Pilatus Turbo-Porter) has been ordered by the USAF as an off-the-shelf "mini gunship" for SE Asia under the "Credible Chase" programme.

FAIRCHILD AU-23A PEACEMAKER

Dimensions: Span, 49 ft 8 in (15,13 m); length, 35 ft 9 in (10,90 m); height, 10 ft 6 in (3,20 m); wing area, 310 sq ft (28,80 m²).

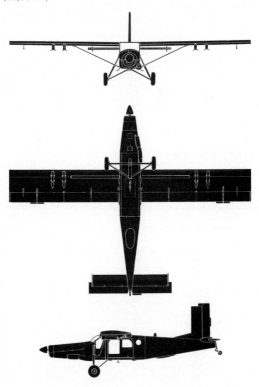

FMA IA 58 PUCARÁ

Country of Origin: Argentina.
Type: Tandem two-seat counter-insurgency aircraft.
Power Plant: Two 1,022 eshp Turboméca Astazou XVIG turboprops.
Performance: Max. speed, 323 mph (520 km/h) at 9,840 ft (3 000 m); max. cruise, 301 mph (485 km/h) at 9,840 ft (3 000 m); econ. cruise, 267 mph (430 km/h); range with two 66 Imp gal (300 l) auxiliary tanks, 1,890 mls (3 040 km) at 16,400 ft (5 000 m); initial climb rate, 3,543 ft/min (18,0 m/sec); service ceiling, 27,165 ft (8 280 m).
Weights: (With TPE-331-U-303 turboprops) Empty equipped, 7,826 lb (3 550 kg); max. take-off, 13,668 lb (6 200 kg).
Armament: Two 20-mm Hispano cannon and four 7,62-mm FN machine guns. One hard point beneath fuselage and one beneath each wing for various combinations of bombs, missiles or weapons pods.
Status: First prototype flown on August 20, 1969, and second prototype on September 6, 1970. An initial production batch of 50 aircraft initiated during 1972.
Notes: First prototype (see 1971 edition) powered by two 904 ehp Garrett AirResearch TPE-331-U-303 turboprops, but second prototype (illustrated) and production aircraft have the Astazou XVIG which has been standardised.

FMA IA 58 PUCARÁ

Dimensions: Span, 47 ft 6¾ in (14,50 m); length, 45 ft 7¼ in (13,90 m); height, 17 ft 2¼ in (5,24 m); wing area, 326·1 sq ft (30,3 m²).

FOKKER F.27 FRIENDSHIP SRS. 500

Country of Origin: Netherlands.

Type: Short- to medium-range commercial transport.

Power Plant: Two 2,250 eshp Rolls-Royce Dart 532-7 turboprops.

Performance: Max. cruise, 322 mph (518 km/h) at 20,000 ft (6 095 m); normal cruise at 38,000 lb (17 237 kg), 298 mph (480 km/h) at 20,000 ft (6 095 m); range with max. payload, 667 mls (1 075 km), with max. fuel and 9,680-lb (4 390-kg) payload, 1,099 mls (1 805 km); initial climb at max. take-off weight, 1,200 ft/min (6,1 m/sec); service ceiling at 38,000 lb (17 237 kg), 29,500 ft (9 000 m).

Weights: Empty, 24,886 lb (11 288 kg); operational empty, 25,951 lb (11 771 kg); max. take-off, 45,000 lb (20 411 kg).

Accommodation: Basic flight crew of two or three and standard seating for 52 passengers. Alternative arrangements for up to 56 passengers.

Status: First Srs. 500 flown November 15, 1967. Production currently standardising on Srs. 500 and 600. Orders for the Friendship (including those licence-built in the USA by Fairchild) totalled 587 by beginning of 1973.

Notes: By comparison with basic Srs. 200 (see 1968 edition), the Srs. 500 has a 4 ft 11 in (1,5 m) fuselage stretch. The Srs. 400 "Combiplane" (see 1966 edition) and the equivalent military Srs. 400M are convertible cargo or combined cargo-passenger versions of the Srs. 200, and the current Srs. 600 is similar to the Srs. 400 but lacks the reinforced and watertight cargo floor.

FOKKER F.27 FRIENDSHIP SRS. 500

Dimensions: Span, 95 ft $1\frac{3}{4}$ in (29,00 m); length, 82 ft $2\frac{1}{2}$ in (25,06 m); height, 28 ft $7\frac{1}{4}$ in (8,71 m); wing area, 753·47 sq ft (70 m²).

FOKKER F.28 FELLOWSHIP MK. 6000

Country of Origin: Netherlands.

Type: Short-range commercial transport.

Power Plant: Two 9,675 lb (4 390 kg) Rolls-Royce Spey Mk. 555-1H turbofans.

Performance: (At 70,000 lb/31 752 kg) 528 mph (849 km/h) at 21,000 ft (6 400 m); long-range cruise, 420 mph (676 km/h) at 30,000 ft (9 150 m); range with max. payload, 1,025 mls (1 650 km), with max. fuel (and 27 passengers), 1,197 mls (1 927 km).

Weights: Operating empty, 37,760 lb (17 127 kg); max. take-off, 70,000 lb (31 752 kg).

Accommodation: Flight crew of two with single-class accommodation for up to 79 passengers in five-abreast seating.

Status: The prototype Fellowship Mk. 6000 (the fuselage of the prototype Mk. 2000 and the modified wings of the second Mk. 1000 prototype) scheduled to fly September 1973.

Notes: The Fellowship Mk. 6000 is a derivative of the stretched-fuselage Mk. 2000 (illustrated above), offering improved field performance and payload/range capabilities. Wing span is increased by 4 ft 11½ in (1,50 m), three-section leading-edge slats are added to each wing, and an uprated, quieter version of the Spey engine is employed. Similar changes to the basic (shorter-fuselage) Fellowship Mk. 1000 will result in the Fellowship Mk. 5000. All four variants of the Fellowship are to be offered in parallel, and a large freight door is to be introduced for cargo or mixed passenger-cargo versions of the Mks 1000 and 5000.

FOKKER F.28 FELLOWSHIP MK. 6000

Dimensions: Span, 82 ft 3¾ in (25,09 m); length, 97 ft 1¼ in (29,61 m); height, 27 ft 9½ in (8,47 m); wing area, 850 sq ft (78,97 m²).

GAF NOMAD

Country of Origin: Australia.
Type: STOL utility transport.
Power Plant: Two 400 eshp Allison 250-B17 turboprops.
Performance: (Nomad 24 at 8,000 lb/3 629 kg) Max. cruise, 199 mph (320 km/h) at sea level, 202 mph (325 km/h) at 5,000 ft (1 524 m); long-range cruise, 161 mph (259 km/h) at 10,000 ft (3 048 m); max. range at 199 mph (320 km/h) at 10,000 ft (3 048 m) with 45 min reserves, 944 mls (1 518 km), with 1,600-lb (726-kg) payload, 725 mls (1 167 km) at max. cruise at sea level; initial climb, 1,500 ft/min (7,62 m/sec); service ceiling, 25,000 ft (7 620 m).
Weights: (Nomad 24) Basic empty, 4,330 lb (1 964 kg); max. take-off, 8,000 lb (3 629 kg).
Accommodation: Flight crew of either one or two, and up to 15 passengers in individual seats.
Status: First and second prototypes of Nomad 22 flown July 23, 1971, and December 5, 1971, respectively. First prototype being converted as Nomad 24 with flight test programme scheduled to commence March 1973. Initial production batch of 20 Nomad 22s with first scheduled to fly late November 1973.
Notes: Nomad 24 (general arrangement drawing) differs from Nomad 22 (second prototype of which is illustrated above) in having plugs in the fuselage fore and aft of the wing. Initial production batch confined to short-fuselage Nomad 22, and GAF (Government Aircraft Factories) to deliver 11 of first batch of 20 to Australian Army Aviation Corps. Military version may feature zero-zero ejection seats for two pilots and armour protection.

GAF NOMAD

Dimensions: Span, 54 ft 0 in (16,46 m); length, 47 ft 0 in (14,30 m(; height, 18 ft 0 in (5,48 m); wing area, 320 sq ft (29,7 m²).

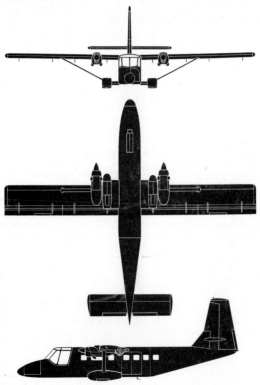

GENERAL DYNAMICS F-111E

Country of Origin: USA.

Type: Two-seat tactical strike fighter.

Power Plant: Two 19,600 lb (8 890 kg) reheat Pratt & Whitney TF30-P-9 turbofans.

Performance: Max. speed, 865 mph (1 390 km/h) or Mach 1·2 at sea level, 1,650 mph (2 655 km/h) or Mach 2·5 at 40,000 ft (12 190 m); ferry range with max. internal fuel, 3,800 mls (6 115 km); tactical radius with 16,000-lb (7 257-kg) combat load for hi-lo-hi mission profile, 1,500 mls (2 415 km).

Weights: Empty operational, 47,500 lb (23 525 kg); normal take-off, 74,000 lb (33 566 kg); max. overload take-off, 91,500 lb (41 504 kg).

Armament: One 20-mm M-61A1 rotary cannon with 2,000 rounds or two 750-lb M117 bombs internally. Approx. max. ordnance load of 30,000 lb (13 608 kg) for short-range interdiction. External ordnance carried by four 4,000-lb (1 814-kg) swivelling wing stations and four fixed stations.

Status: First of 28 test and development F-111s flown December 21, 1964. Initial production model, the F-111A (see 1969 edition), of which 141 built. Superseded by F-111E (94 aircraft) from late 1969, these being followed by F-111D (96 aircraft) and F-111F (82 aircraft), with production phase-out December 1973.

Notes: F-111E differs from F-111A in having revised air intake geometry and TF30-P-9 turbofans, and the similarly-powered F-111D features more advanced avionics. The F-111F has TF30-P-100 engines and simplified avionics. Production of a strategic bombing version, the FB-111A (see 1972 edition), terminated in 1971.

GENERAL DYNAMICS F-111E

Dimensions: Span (max.), 63 ft 0 in (19,20 m), (min.), 31 ft 11⅓ in (9,74); length, 73 ft 6 in (∠2,40 m); height, 17 ft 1⅓ in (5,22 m).

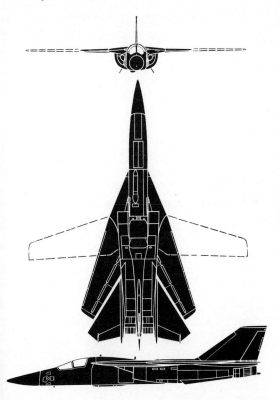

GRUMMAN A-6 INTRUDER

Country of Origin: USA.
Type: Two-seat shipboard low-level strike aircraft.
Power Plant: Two 9,300 lb (4 218 kg) Pratt & Whitney J52-P-8A turbojets.
Performance: Max. speed at 36,655 lb (16 626 kg) in clean condition, 685 mph (1 102 km/h) or Mach 0·9 at sea level, 625 mph (1 006 km/h) or Mach 0·94 at 36,000 ft (10 970 m); average cruise, 480 mph (772 km/h) at 32,750–43,800 ft (9 980–13 350 m); range with max. internal fuel and four Bullpup ASMs, 1,920 mls (3 090 km), with single store and four 250 Imp gal (1 136 l) external tanks, 3,040 mls (4 890 km).
Weights: Empty, 25,684 lb (11 650 kg); loaded (clean), 37,116 lb (16 836 kg); max. overload take-off, 60,280 lb (27 343 kg).
Armament: Max. external ordnance load of 15,000 lb (6 804 kg) distributed between five 3,600-lb (1 633-kg) stores stations.
Status: First of eight test and development aircraft flown April 19, 1960 and first delivery to US Navy (A-6A) on February 7, 1963.
Notes: Specification relates to basic A-6A (see 1970 edition), drawing depicts A-6B which differs in having equipment for AGM-78A Standard ARM (Anti-Radiation Missile), the A-6C has a detachable ventral turret for low-light television and infra-red sensors, and the KA-6D is a shipboard tanker version. The A-6E has more advanced avionics and flew in prototype form on February 27, 1970, first deliveries to the US Navy following in 1971.

GRUMMAN A-6 INTRUDER

Dimensions: Span, 53 ft 0 in (16,15 m); length, 54 ft 7 in (16,64 m); height, 15 ft 7 in (4,75 m); wing area, 529 sq ft (49,15 m²).

GRUMMAN EA-6B PROWLER

Country of Origin: USA.

Type: Four-seat shipboard electronic warfare aircraft.

Power Plant: Two 9,300 lb (4 218 kg) Pratt & Whitney J52-P-8A turbojets.

Performance: Max. speed, 599 mph (964 km/h) at sea level; average cruise, 466 mph (750 km/h); ferry range (with five 250 Imp gal/1 136 l external tanks), 2,475 mls (3 982 km); service ceiling, 38,000 ft (11 582 m).

Weights: Empty, 34,581 lb (15 686 kg); typical mission, 51,000 lb (23 133 kg); max. take-off, 58,500 lb (26 535 kg); max. overload, 63,177 lb (28 656 lb).

Accommodation: Forward cockpit housing pilot and electronic countermeasures operator side-by-side, and aft cockpit providing side-by-side seating for two additional countermeasures operators.

Status: Prototype EA-6B flown May 25, 1968, with first production deliveries to US Navy following in January 1971 with operational deployment commencing mid-1972. Total procurement of approximately 40 EA-6Bs by the US Navy anticipated.

Notes: Derived from the A-6 Intruder (see pages 100–101), the Prowler is intended to intercept, analyse, evaluate and jam hostile radar emissions. The primary mission is tactical stand-off jamming, and the Prowler carries 8,000 lb (3 629 kg) of avionics internally and a 950-lb (431-kg) avionics pod on the fuselage centreline and on four wing stations. The Prowler can also be used in the ECM escort or penetration roles, and its range and altitude are compatible with the A-6 Intruder.

GRUMMAN EA-6B PROWLER

Dimensions: Span, 53 ft 0 in (16,15 m); length, 59 ft 5 in (18,11 m); height, 16 ft 3 in (4,95 m); wing area, 529 sq ft (49,15 m²).

GRUMMAN F-14A TOMCAT

Country of Origin: USA.

Type: Two-seat shipboard multi-purpose fighter.

Power Plant: Two (approx) 20,600 lb (9 344 kg) reheat Pratt & Whitney TF30-P-412 turbofans.

Performance: (Estimated) Max. speed with four AIM-7 Sparrow missiles for intercept mission at approx. 57,300 lb (25 990 kg), 910 mph (1 470 km/h) or Mach 1·2 at sea level, 1,564 mph (2 517 km/h) or Mach 2·34 at 40,000 ft (12 190 m).

Weights: (Estimated) Empty, 37,500 lb. (17 010 kg); normal take-off (intercept mission), 57,300 lb (25 990 kg); max. take-off, 66,200 lb (30 028 kg).

Armament: One 20-mm M-61A1 rotary cannon and (intercept mission) four AIM-7 Sparrow and four AIM-9 Sidewinder AAMs or six AIM-54 Phoenix and two AIM-9 AAMs.

Status: First of 12 research and development aircraft commenced flight trials on December 21, 1970, followed by second on May 24, 1971. US Navy anticipated total buy of 301 F-14 series fighters at beginning of 1973.

Notes: F-14A is to attain operational status in 1973, the first two squadrons to fly the Tomcat having been activated in October 1972. It is anticipated that the 123rd and subsequent aircraft will be completed to F-14B standard with advanced technology Pratt & Whitney F401-PW-401 turbofans of some 30,000 lb (13 610 kg), increasing thrust/weight ratio from 0·84 to 1·16, estimated acceleration from Mach 0·8 to Mach 1·8 being 1·27 minutes. The F-14B is expected to commence fleet indoctrination late 1974 or early 1975. The proposed F-14C version of the Tomcat embodies a more advanced avionics system.

GRUMMAN F-14A TOMCAT

Dimensions: Span (max.), 62 ft 10 in (19,15 m), (min.), 37 ft 7 in (11,45 m); length, 61 ft 10½ in (18,86 m); height, 16 ft 0 in (4,88 m).

GRUMMAN AMERICAN AVIATION
AA-5 TRAVELER

Country of Origin: USA.
Type: Light cabin monoplane.
Power Plant: One 150 hp Avco Lycoming O-320-E2G four-cylinder horizontally-opposed engine.
Performance: Max. speed, 150 mph (241 km/h) at sea level; cruise (75% power), 140 mph (225 km/h) at 9,000 ft (2 743 m); range at 9,000 ft (2 743 m) without reserves, 600 mls (966 km) at 75% power, 645 mls (1 038 km) at 65% power; initial climb, 660 ft/min (3,35 m/sec); service ceiling, 12,650 ft (3 856 m).
Weights: Empty equipped, 1,304 lb (592 kg); max. take-off, 2,200 lb (998 kg).
Accommodation: Pilot and three passengers in paired separate seats beneath aft-sliding canopy.
Status: The prototype AA-5 Traveler was first flown on August 21, 1970, production deliveries following on FAA certification in December 1971. Combined production rate of AA-5 and AA-1A Trainer (which have some 60% commonality) was approx. 50 per month at beginning of 1973.
Notes: The AA-5 Traveler is essentially an enlarged version of the side-by-side two-seat AA-1A Trainer (see 1972 edition) and is currently being produced by Grumman American Aviation, formed in 1972 by the merger of the civil aircraft interests of Grumman with American Aviation.

GRUMMAN AMERICAN AVIATION AA-5 TRAVELER

Dimensions: Span, 31 ft 6 in (9,60 m); length, 22 ft 6¾ in (6,87 m); height, 8 ft 2½ in (2,50 m); wing area, 140 sq ft 13,01 m²).

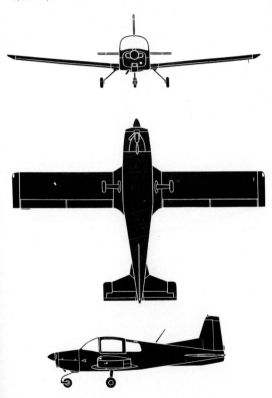

HAL HA-31 MK. II BASANT

Country of Origin: India.

Type: Single-seat agricultural monoplane.

Power Plant: One 400 hp Avco Lycoming IO-720-C1B six-cylinder horizontally-opposed engine.

Performance: Max. speed (at 5,004 lb/2 270 kg), 147 mph (237 km/h) at sea level, (at 4,332 lb/1 965 kg), 151 mph (243 km/h); initial climb rate (at 4,332 lb/1 965 kg), 1,066 ft/min (5,4 m/sec); service ceiling, 14,900 ft (4 540 m).

Weights: Empty equipped, 2,579 lb (1 170 kg); max. take-off (normal), 4,332 lb (1 965 kg), (restricted), 5,004 lb (2 270 kg).

Status: First of two prototypes of the HA-31 Mk. II flown March 30, 1972, with second following mid-September 1972. Production scheduled to commence during 1973 against initial Ministry of Agriculture requirement for 200 aircraft.

Notes: The HA-31 Mk. II bears no design relationship to the single-seat agricultural monoplane flown in 1969 under the designation HA-31 and subsequently abandoned. The hopper for dry or liquid pesticides or fertilisers is installed between the engine firewall and the front wall of the cockpit and has a maximum capacity of 2,006 lb (910 kg) for restricted category operation or 1,333 lb (605 kg) for normal category operation. Safety provisions include an impact-absorbing structure ahead of the cockpit. The Basant features a steel tube airframe with fabric skinning apart from the engine cowling and hopper which are metal covered. It is cleared for an ultimate load factor of 6·3*g* in the normal category.

HAL HA-31 MK. II BASANT

Dimensions: Span, 39 ft 4½in (11,99 m); length, 29 ft 6½ in (9,00 m); height, 8 ft 4½ in (2,55 m); wing area, 251 sq ft (23,34 m²).

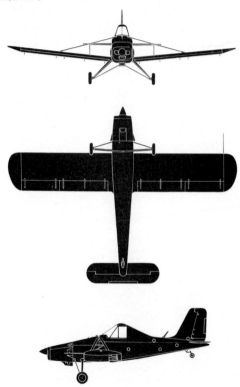

HAWKER SIDDELEY 125 SERIES 600

Country of Origin: United Kingdom.
Type: Light business executive transport.
Power Plant: Two 3,750 lb (1 700 kg) Rolls-Royce Viper 601 turbojets.
Performance: Max. cruise, 518 mph (834 km/h) at 27,000 ft (8 230 m); long-range cruise, 503 mph (810 km/h) at 40,000 ft (12 192 m); range (max. fuel and 1,600-lb/725-kg payload plus 45 min reserves), 1,876 mls (3 020 km), (with 2,359-lb/1 070-kg payload), 1,785 mls (2 872 km); max. initial climb, 4,900 ft/min (24,89 m/sec).
Weights: Empty equipped, 12,148 lb (5 510 kg); max. take-off, 25,000 lb (11 340 kg).
Accommodation: Normal flight crew of two and basic arrangement for eight passengers with alternative arrangements available for up to 14 passengers.
Status: Two Series 600 development aircraft flown on January 21, 1971, and November 25, 1971. Production deliveries scheduled to commence January 1973.
Notes: The Series 600 is the current production version of the basic HS.125, this being essentially a higher-powered, stretched version of the Series 400 which it replaces. An additional 2-ft (0,62-m) section has been inserted in the fuselage ahead of the wing leading edge, this allowing two more seats to be offered in the cabin; a nose radome of improved profile has been adopted; the upper fuselage contours have been revised, and taller vertical tail surfaces have been adopted. Aircraft completed to US standards are being marketed in the USA by Beech as the BH.125-600A.

HAWKER SIDDELEY 125 SERIES 600

Dimensions: Span, 47 ft 0 in (14,32 m); length, 50 ft 5¾ in (15,37 m); height, 17 ft 3 in (5,26 m); wing area, 353 sq ft (32,8 m²).

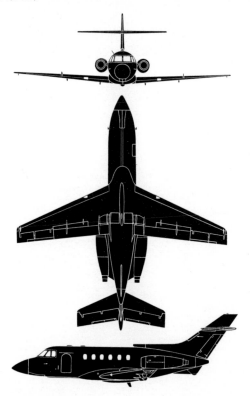

HAWKER SIDDELEY 748 SERIES 2A

Country of Origin: United Kingdom.
Type: Short- to medium-range commercial transport.
Power Plant: Two 2,280 ehp Rolls-Royce Dart R.Da.7 Mk. 532-2L turboprops.
Performance: Max. speed at 40,000 lb (18 145 kg), 312 mph (502 km/h) at 16,000 ft (4 875 m); max. cruise, 287 mph (462 km/h) at 15,000 ft (4 570 m); econ. cruise, 267 mph (430 km/h) at 20,000 ft (6 095 m); range cruise, 259 mph (418 km/h) at 25,000 ft (7 620 m); range with max. fuel and reserves for 45 min hold and 230-mile (370-km) diversion, 1,862 mls (2 996 km), with max. payload and same reserves, 690 mls (1 110 km).
Weights: Basic operational, 25,361 lb (11 504 kg); max. take-off, 44,495 lb (20 182 kg).
Accommodation: Normal flight crew of two and standard cabin arrangement for 40 passengers in paired seats. Alternative high-density arrangement for 58 passengers.
Status: First prototype flown June 24, 1960, and first production model (Series 1) on August 30, 1961. Series 1 superseded by Series 2 in 1962, this being in turn superseded by current Series 2A from mid-1967. Total of 263 ordered by beginning of 1973.
Notes: Manufactured under licence in India by HAL for Indian Airlines (24) and Indian Air Force (five Series 1 and 40 Series 2) at rate of nine per year, 45 having been delivered by beginning of 1973. The Series 2C (illustrated above) flown on December 31, 1971, is similar to the Series 2A apart from the addition of a large rear freight door.

HAWKER SIDDELEY 748 SERIES 2A

Dimensions: Span, 98 ft 6 in (30,02 m); length, 67 ft 0 in (20,42 m); height, 24 ft 10 in (7,57 m); wing area, 810·75 sq ft (75,35 m²).

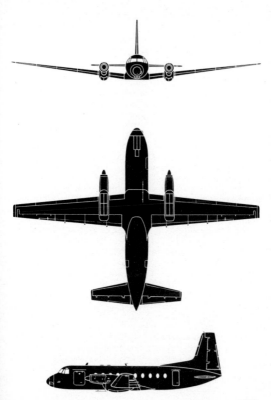

HAWKER SIDDELEY BUCCANEER
S. MK. 2B

Country of Origin: United Kingdom.

Type: Two-seat strike and reconnaissance aircraft.

Power Plant: Two 11,100 lb (5 035 kg) Rolls-Royce RB. 168-1A Spey Mk. 101 turbofans.

Performance: (Estimated) Max. speed, 645 mph (1 040 km/h) or Mach 0·85 at 250 ft (75 m), 620 mph (998 km/h) or Mach 0·92 at 30,000 ft (9 145 m); typical low-level cruise, 570 mph (917 km/h) or Mach 0·75 at 3,000 ft (915 m); tactical radius for hi-lo-lo-hi mission with standard fuel, 500–600 mls (805–965 km).

Weights: Max. take-off, 59,000 lb (26 762 kg).

Armament: Max. ordnance load of 16,000 lb (7 257 kg), including four 500-lb (227-kg), 540-lb (245-kg), or 1,000-lb (453,5-kg) bombs internally, and up to three 1,000-lb (453,5-kg) or six 500-lb (227-kg) bombs on each of four wing stations.

Status: First S. Mk. 2B for RAF flown January 8, 1970, with deliveries of 42 built to this standard continuing into 1973. Proportion of 84 S. Mk. 2s built for Royal Navy being modified for RAF use as S. Mk. 2As, and most of these ultimately to be converted to S. Mk. 2Bs.

Notes: The S. Mk. 2A embodies avionic, system and equipment modifications for RAF service. Wing and weapon-pylon changes to provide Martel missile capability characterise the S. Mk. 2B which introduces 425 Imp gal (1 932 l) fuel tank on rotating bomb door (seen on accompanying drawing) and undercarriage changes to accommodate new gross weight of 59,000 lb (26 762 kg). The Royal Navy versions are the S. Mk. 2C and S. Mk. 2D without and with Martel capability respectively.

HAWKER SIDDELEY BUCCANEER S. MK. 2B

Dimensions: Span, 44 ft 0 in (13,41 m); length, 63 ft 5 in (19,33 m); height, 16 ft 3 in (4,95 m); wing area, 514·7 sq ft (47,82 m²).

HAWKER SIDDELEY HARRIER G.R. MK. 3

Country of Origin: United Kingdom.
Type: Single-seat V/STOL strike and reconnaissance fighter.
Power Plant: One 21,500 lb (9 760 kg) Rolls-Royce Bristol Pegasus 103 vectored-thrust turbofan.
Performance: Max. speed, 720 mph (1 160 km/h) or Mach 0·95 at 1,000 ft (305 m), with typical external ordnance load, 640–660 mph (1 030–1 060 km) or Mach 0·85–0·87 at 1,000 ft (305 m); cruise, 560 mph (900 km/h) or Mach 0·8 at 20,000 ft (6 096 m); tactical radius for hi-lo-hi mission, 260 mls (418 km), with two 100 Imp gal (455 l) external tanks, 400 mls (644 km); ferry range with four 330 Imp gal (1 500 l) external tanks, 2,070 mls (3 330 km).
Weights: Empty, 12,400 lb (5 624 kg); max. take-off (VTO), 18,000 lb (8 165 kg); max. take-off (STO), 23,000+ lb (10 433+ kg); approx. max. take-off, 26,000 lb (11 793 kg).
Armament: Provision for two 30-mm Aden cannon with 130 rpg and up to 5,000 lb (2 268 kg) of ordnance on five external hardpoints.
Status: First of six pre-production aircraft flown August 31, 1966, with first of 77 G.R. Mk. 1s for RAF following December 28, 1967. Production of G.R. Mk. 1s and 13 T. Mk. 2s (see 1969 edition) for RAF completed. Production of 114 Mk. 50s (equivalent to G.R. Mk. 3) for US Marine Corps continuing through 1973, first having been delivered January 26, 1971.
Notes: RAF Harrier G.R. Mk. 1s and T. Mk. 2s converted to G. R. Mk. 1As and T. Mk. 2As by installation of 20,000 lb (9 100 kg) Pegasus 102. These are to be progressively modified as G.R. Mk. 3s and T. Mk. 4s by installation of Pegasus 103 similar to that installed in Mk. 50 (AV-8A) for USMC. The G.R. Mk. 3s are to be fitted with nose-mounted laser rangefinder, new nose shape being illustrated above.

Dimensions: Span, 25 ft 3 in (7,70 m); length, 45 ft 7¾ in (13,91 m); height, 11 ft 3 in (3,43 m); wing area, 201·1 sq ft (18,68 m²).

HAWKER SIDDELEY NIMROD M.R. MK. 1

Country of Origin: United Kingdom.
Type: Long-range maritime patrol aircraft.
Power Plant: Four (approx) 11,500 lb (5 217 kg) Rolls-Royce RB. 168-20 Spey Mk. 250 turbofans.
Performance: Max. speed, 575 mph (926 km/h); max. transit speed, 547 mph (880 km/h); econ. transit speed, 490 mph (787 km/h); typical ferry range, 5,180–5,755 mls (8 340-9 265 km); typical endurance, 12 hrs.
Weights: Typical take-off, 175,500 lb (79 605 kg); max. take-off, 192,000 lb (87 090 kg).
Armament: Ventral weapons bay accommodating full range of ASW weapons (homing torpedoes, mines, depth charges, etc) and two underwing pylons for AS.12 ASMs.
Accommodation: Normal flight crew of three on flight deck with nine navigators and sensor operators in tactical compartment. Provision is made for conversion for the trooping role and in this configuration up to 45 troops may be accommodated in the rear pressure cabin.
Status: First of two Nimrod prototypes employing modified Comet 4C airframes flown May 23, 1967. First of initial batch of 38 production Nimrod M.R. Mk. 1s flown on June 28, 1968, followed by first delivery to RAF on October 2, 1969. M.R. Mk. 1s followed by three Nimrod R. Mk. 1s for special reconnaissance duties. Initial RAF order completed 1971, but a supplementary contract for a further eight M.R. Mk. 1s was placed early in 1972.
Notes: The world's first shore-based turbojet-propelled maritime patrol aircraft, the Nimrod employs the basic structure of the Comet 4C transport (see 1963 edition) and is equipping five RAF squadrons.

118

HAWKER SIDDELEY NIMROD M.R. MK. 1

Dimensions: Span, 114 ft 10 in (35,00 m); length, 126 ft 9 in (38,63 m); height, 29 ft 8½ in (9,01 m); wing area, 2,121 sq ft (197,05 m²).

HAWKER SIDDELEY TRIDENT 3B

Country of Origin: United Kingdom.
Type: Short-haul commercial transport.
Power Plant: Three 11,930 lb (5 411 kg) Rolls-Royce RB.163–25 Mk. 512-5W turbofans plus one 5,250 lb (2 381 kg) Rolls-Royce RB.162-86 turbojet.
Performance: Max. cruise, 601 mph (967 km/h) at 28,300 ft (8 625 m); econ. cruise, 533 mph (858 km/h) at 29,000–33,000 ft (8 000–10 000 m); typical high-speed cruise, 581 mph (936 km/h) at 25,000 ft (7 620 m); range with max. payload and reserves for 250 mls (402 km) and 45 min hold, 1,658 mls (2 668 km), with max. payload and same reserves, 1,094 mls (1 760 km).
Weights: Operational empty as 128-seater, 83,473 lb (37 863 kg), as 152-seater, 83,104 lb (37 695 kg); max. take-off, 150,000 lb (68 040 kg).
Accommodation: Basic flight crew of three and alternative arrangements for 14 first-class and 114 tourist-class passengers, or 152 tourist-class passengers. High-density arrangements for 164 or 171 passengers.
Status: First Trident 3B flown December 11, 1969. Twenty-six ordered for BEA, with which airline the Trident 3B entered service on April 1, 1971.
Notes: The Trident 3B is a high-capacity short-haul development of the Trident 1E (see 1966 edition) with a stretched fuselage and similar power plants and wing modifications to those of the Trident 2E (see 1969 edition). The latter is still in production, 18 having been ordered by China, together with two Super Trident 3Bs. The 3B also embodies wing area, wing incidence, and flap span increases, and an RB.162-86 auxiliary turbojet beneath the tail.

HAWKER SIDDELEY TRIDENT 3B

Dimensions: Span, 98 ft 0 in (29,87 m); length, 131 ft 2 in (39,98 m); height, 28 ft 3 in (8,61 m); wing area, 1,493 sq ft (138,7 m²).

HELIO AU-24A STALLION

Country of Origin: USA.

Type: Light counter-insurgency and utility aircraft.

Power Plant: One 680 shp Pratt & Whitney (UACL) PT6A-27 turboprop.

Performance: Max. speed (at 5,100 lb/2 313 kg), 216 mph (348 km/h) at 10,000 ft (3 050 m); max. cruise, 206 mph (332 km/h) at 10,000 ft (3 050 m); econ. cruise, 160 mph (257 km/h); initial climb, 2,200 ft/min (11,18 m/sec); service ceiling, 28,000 ft (8 530 m); max. range, 1,090 mls (1 755 km).

Weights: Empty equipped, 2,860 lb (1 297 kg); normal loaded, 5,100 lb (2 313 kg); max. overload, 6,300 lb (2 858 kg).

Armament: One side-firing flexibly-mounted 20-mm XM-197 cannon plus various ordnance loads on one under-fuselage and four underwing hardpoints. Up to 500-lb (227 kg) may be carried beneath the fuselage, 600 lb (272 kg) on each inner wing hardpoint and 300 lb (136 kg) on each outer hardpoint.

Accommodation: Pilot and co-pilot or passenger side-by-side in front. Freight or six–nine passengers may be carried in the utility role.

Status: Two prototype AU-24As followed in 1972 by evaluation batch of 15 aircraft.

Notes: The AU-24A is a ''mini gunship'' version of the commercial H-550A Stallion which was being evaluated by the USAF during 1972 in competition with the Fairchild AU-23A Peacemaker (see pages 88–89) under the ''Credible Chase'' programme.

HELIO AU-24A STALLION

Dimensions: Span, 41 ft 0 in (12,50 m); length, 39 ft 7 in (12,07 m); height, 9 ft 3 in (2,81 m); wing area, 242 sq ft (22,48 m²).

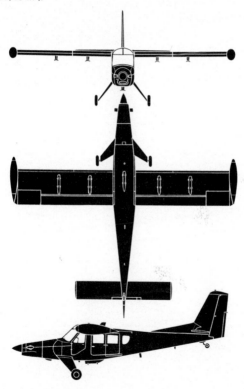

IAI-201 ARAVA

Country of Origin: Israel.

Type: Light Military transport and gunship.

Power Plant: Two 783 eshp Pratt & Whitney (UACL) PT6A-34 turboprops.

Performance: Max. speed (at 15,000 lb/6 803 kg), 203 mph (326 km/h) at 10,000 ft (3 050 m); max. cruise, 198 mph (319 km/h) at 10,000 ft (3 050 m); econ. cruise, 193 mph (311 km/h); max. range (with 45 min reserves), 806 mls (1 297 km); range with max. payload, 201 mls (323 km); initial climb, 1,564 ft/min (7,09 m/sec); service ceiling, 26,575 ft (8 100 m).

Weights: Empty equipped, 7,787 lb (3 532 kg); max. take-off, 15,000 lb (6 803 kg).

Armament: One 0·5-in (12,7-mm) machine gun on each side of fuselage with 250 rpg, and provision for single aft-firing 0·5-in (12,7-mm) gun in flexible mount in the fuselage tail. Two hardpoints on fuselage are of 600-lb (272-kg) capacity and may carry such offensive stores as six-round 82-mm rocket pods.

Accommodation: Flight crew of one or two plus 23 fully-equipped troops or 16 paratroops and two despatchers. Eight casualty stretchers and three sitting casualties.

Status: Prototype IAI-201 began flight testing late 1971, and production at rate of one per month planned for 1973.

Notes: The IAI-201 is a military derivative of the IAI-101 (see 1972 edition), the former currently having production priority over the latter.

IAI-201 ARAVA

Dimensions: Span, 69 ft 6 in (20,88 m); length, 42 ft 7½ in (12,99 m); height, 17 ft 0¾ in (5,20 m); wing area, 470·2 sq ft (43,68 m²).

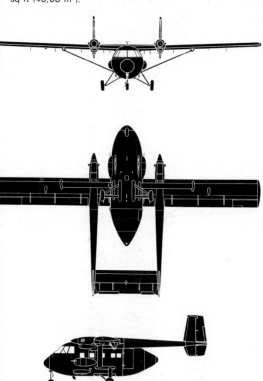

ICA IS-24

Country of Origin: Romania.
Type: Light cabin monoplane.
Power Plant: One 290 hp Lycoming IO-540-G1C5 six-cylinder horizontally-opposed engine.
Performance: Max. speed, 137 mph (220 km/h) at sea level; max. cruise, 124 mph (200 km/h) at sea level; max. range, 435 mls (700 km); initial climb rate, 787 ft/min (4,0 m/sec).
Weights: Empty equipped, 2,733 lb (1 240 kg); max. take-off, 4,188 lb (1 900 kg).
Accommodation: Pilot and five passengers in three pairs of side-by-side seats. Two stretchers may be carried for the aeromedical role.
Status: The prototype IS-24 commenced its flight test programme late in 1971 and series production is envisaged for 1973.
Notes: Built by the Intreprinderea de Constructii Aeronautice (ICA) of Brasov, and designed by Ing Iosif Silimon, the IS-24 has been evolved from the experimental IS-23-A (see 1969 edition) and is intended to fulfil a variety of roles, including the training of parachutists, photographic survey, and glider towing. In the last-mentioned role the IS-24 is capable of towing two gliders simultaneously. Several derivatives of the IS-24 are projected, such as a STOL version with extensive high-lift devices, including two-section ailerons and slotted Fowler-type flaps on each wing, and a twin-float seaplane variant.

ICA IS-24

Dimensions: Span, 40 ft 8¼ in (12,40 m); length, 30 ft 2½ in (9,20 m); height, 10 ft 10 in (3,30 m); wing area, 250·8 sq ft (23,30 m²).

ILYUSHIN IL-62M-200 (CLASSIC)

Country of Origin: USSR.

Type: Long-range commercial transport.

Power Plant: Four 25,350 lb (11 500 kg) Soloviev D-30-KU turbofans.

Performance: Max. cruise, 560 mph (900 km/h) at 39,400 ft (12 000 m); range cruise, 528 mph (850 km/h) at 36,090 ft (11 000 m); range with max. payload and reserves, 4,970 mls (8 000 km), with max. fuel, 6,400 mls (10 300 km).

Weights: Max. take-off, 363,760 lb (165 000 kg).

Accommodation: Normal flight crew of five, and alternative configurations for 198 economy class, 186 tourist class or 161 mixed class passengers.

Status: First of two prototypes of the Il-62 flown January 1963, these being followed by three pre-production aircraft. Deliveries of basic Il-62 (to Aeroflot) began 1967, and developed Il-62M-200 is scheduled to enter service during 1973 on Aeroflot's Moscow—New York service, eventually replacing the earlier Il-62 on all of Aeroflot's longer-range routes.

Notes: The Il-62M-200, which appeared in 1971, differs from the basic Il-62 in having the 23,150 lb (10 500 kg) Kuznetsov NK-8-4 turbofans replaced by D-30-KU engines, and a small increase in passenger capacity achieved by re-arrangement of the toilet and wardrobe areas at the rear of the cabin. Other changes include the provision of a containerised baggage and freight system with mechanised loading and unloading, clam-shell thrust reversers on the outboard engines, and an additional fuel tank in the tailfin of 1,100 Imp gal (5 000 l) capacity. The flight deck has been revised and new communications and navigational equipment introduced.

ILYUSHIN IL-62M-200 (CLASSIC)

Dimensions: Span, 139 ft 5¼ in (42,50 m); length, 174 ft 2½ in (53,12 m); height, 40 ft 6¼ in (12,35 m); wing area, 3,008·5 sq ft (279,5 m²).

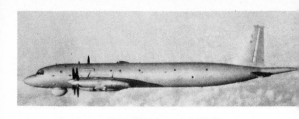

ILYUSHIN IL-38 (MAY)

Country of Origin: USSR.

Type: Long-range maritime patrol aircraft.

Power Plant: Four 4,250 ehp Ivchenko AI-20M turboprops.

Performance: (Estimated) Max. continuous cruise, 400 mph (645 km/h) at 15,000 ft (4 570 m); normal cruise, 370 mph (595 km/h) at 26,250 ft (8 000 m); patrol speed, 250 mph (400 km/h) at 2,000 ft (610 m); max. range, 4,500 mls (7 240 km); loiter endurance, 12 hrs at 2,000 ft (610 m).

Weights: (Estimated) Empty equipped, 80,000 lb (36 287 kg); max. take-off, 140,000 lb (63 500 kg).

Armament: Internal weapons bay for depth bombs, homing torpedoes, etc. Wing hardpoints for external ordnance loads.

Accommodation: Normal flight crew believed to consist of 12 members, of which half are housed by tactical compartment.

Status: The Il-38 reportedly flew in prototype form during 1967–68, entering service with the Soviet naval air arm early in 1970.

Notes: The Il-38 has been evolved from the Il-18 commercial transport in a similar fashion to the development of the Lockheed P-3 Orion from the Electra transport. Apart from some strengthening, the wings, tail assembly and undercarriage are similar to those of the Il-18, these items having been married to an entirely new fuselage housing antisubmarine warfare systems, a tactical operations compartment and weapons bays, terminating in a MAD (Magnetic Anomaly Detection) tail "sting". By comparison with the Il-18, the wing is positioned further forward on the fuselage for CG reasons.

ILYUSHIN IL-38 (MAY)

Dimensions: Span, 122 ft 9 in (37,40 m); length, 131 ft 0 in (39,92 m); height, 33 ft 4 in (10,17 m); wing area, 1,507 sq ft (140,0 m²).

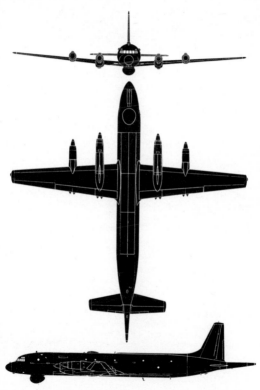

ILYUSHIN IL-76 (CANDID)

Country of Origin: USSR.
Type: Heavy commercial and military freighter.
Power Plant: Four 26,455 lb (12 000 kg) Soloviev D-30-KP turbofans.
Performance: Max. cruise, 528 mph (850 km/h) at 42,650 ft (13 000 m); range with max. payload, 3,107 mls (5 000 km).
Weights: Max. take-off, 346,122 lb (157 000 kg).
Accommodation: Normal flight crew of three—four on flight deck and in glazed nose, and pressurised hold for freight.
Status: Prototype flown for the first time on March 25, 1971, with production deliveries likely to commence in 1973–74.
Notes: Apparently evolved primarily to meet a military requirement, the Il-76 is generally similar in concept to the Lockheed C-141A StarLifter, but is slightly larger, more powerful and heavier. It employs a mechanised cargo-handling system, a high-flotation undercarriage, the main members of which comprise four individual units each of four parallel-mounted wheels, and extensive high-lift devices to achieve short-field performance. According to an official Soviet statement, the Il-76 is intended to operate from short unprepared strips in Siberia and other undeveloped areas of the Soviet Union during the period of the current five-year programme (1971–75). Clam-shell thrust reversers are fitted to all four power plants.

ILYUSHIN IL-76 (CANDID)

Dimensions: Span, 165 ft 8$\frac{1}{2}$ in (50,50 m); length, 152 ft 10$\frac{1}{4}$ in (46,59 m); height, 48 ft 5$\frac{1}{8}$ in (14,76 m).

ITALAIR F.20 PEGASO

Country of Origin: Italy.

Type: Light business executive aircraft.

Power Plant: Two 300 hp Continental IO-520-F six-cylinder horizontally-opposed engines.

Performance: Max. speed, 250 mph (402 km/h) at sea level; cruise (75% power), 236 mph (380 km/h) at 8,000 ft (2 440 m), (65% power), 230 mph (370 km/h) at 10,000 ft (3 050 m); econ. cruise (50% power), 212 mph (340 km/h) at 13,000 ft (3 960 m); max. range (75% power), 1,050 mls (1 690 km), (60% power), 1,270 mls (2 045 km); initial climb, 2,200 ft/min (11,17 m/sec); service ceiling, 20,400 ft (6 220 m).

Weights: Empty equipped, 3,250 lb (1 474 kg); max. take-off, 5,071 lb (2 300 kg).

Accommodation: Seating for up to six persons (including pilot) in three pairs of side-by-side seats. Full dual controls and provision for up to 150 lb (68 kg) of baggage.

Status: First of two prototypes flown on October 21, 1971, with second and revised (to production standards) prototype following on August 11, 1972. Ten production aircraft under construction by Italair at the beginning of 1973.

Notes: The Pegaso (Pegasus) has been designed by Stelio Frati of Costruzioni Aeronautiche General Avia, which company built the prototypes, and production is being undertaken by Italair. The second prototype (illustrated on these pages) embodies the changes being incorporated in the production model.

ITALAIR F.20 PEGASO

Dimensions: Span, 33 ft 9 in (10,28 m); length, 26 ft 5⅔ in (8,06 m); height, 11 ft 5¾ in (3,50 m); wing area, 172·43 sq ft (16,02 m²).

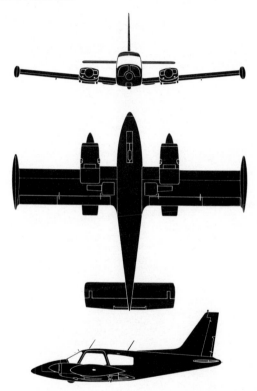

KAWASAKI XC-1A

Country of Origin: Japan.

Type: Medium-range military transport.

Power Plant: Two 14,500 lb (6 575 kg) Pratt & Whitney JT8D-9 turbofans.

Performance: (Estimated) Max. speed, 507 mph (815 km/h) at 23,200 ft (7 600 m); max. cruise, 438 mph (704 km/h) at 35,100 ft (10 700 m); range with max. fuel, 2,073 mls (3 335 km), with (normal) 17,637-lb (8 000-kg) payload, 806 mls (1 297 km); initial climb, 3,806 ft/min (19,3 m/sec); service ceiling, 39,370 ft (12 000 m).

Weights: Empty equipped, 50,706 lb (23 000 kg); max. take-off, 85,980 lb (39 000 kg).

Accommodation: Basic crew of five. Loads include 60 troops, 45 paratroops, or 36 casualty stretchers plus medical attendants. Cargo loads may include a 5,000-lb (2 268-kg) truck, a 105-mm howitzer, two 1,500-lb (680-kg) trucks, or three jeep-type vehicles.

Status: First of two flying prototypes flown on November 12, 1970, and second on January 16, 1971. Production deliveries scheduled to commence during the 1974 fiscal year in which three will be delivered to the Air Self-Defence Force. A further eight C-1As are expected to be delivered during the 1975 fiscal year against total procurement of 24 aircraft during the current (1972–75) five-year defence programme.

Notes: The C-1A is intended as a successor to the Curtiss C-46 transport and an airborne early-warning derivative is expected to fly in 1977.

KAWASAKI XC-1A

Dimensions: Span, 101 ft 8½ in (31,00 m); length, 95 ft 1¾ in (29,00 m); height, 32 ft 9¾ in (10,00 m); wing area, 1,291·7 sq ft (120 m²).

LET L 410 TURBOLET

Country of Origin: Czechoslovakia.
Type: Light utility transport and feederliner.
Power Plant: Two 715 eshp Pratt & Whitney PT6A-27 turboprops.
Performance: Max. cruise, 229 mph (370 km/h) at 9,840 ft (3 000 m); econ. cruise, 205 mph (330 km/h) at 9,840 ft (3 000 m); range with max. fuel and 45 min reserves, 705 mls (1 140 km), with max. payload and same reserves, 115 mls (185 km); initial climb rate, 1,595 ft/min (8,1 m/sec); service ceiling, 25,490 ft (7 770 m).
Weights: Empty equipped, 6,180 lb (2 803 kg); max. take-off, 11,245 lb (5 100 kg).
Accommodation: Basic flight crew of two. Configurations for 12, 15, 19 or 20 passengers in rows of three with two seats to starboard and one to port of aisle. Business executive layout available with accommodation for eight passengers.
Status: First of four prototypes flown April 16, 1969. Pre-production series of six aircraft built during 1971 of which two entered service with Slovak Air in September of that year. First production deliveries (to CSA) commenced in 1972.
Notes: Principal production version of the Turbolet is to receive indigenous M-601-B turboprop of 740 eshp with which it was scheduled to commence flight testing during 1971. Latest modifications (see drawing) include redesigned wheel sponsons, a wider undercarriage track and revised engine nacelles.

LET L 410 TURBOLET

Dimensions: Span, 56 ft 1¼ in (17,10 m); length, 44 ft 7½ in (13,61 m); height, 18 ft 0½ in (5,50 m); wing area, 349·827 sq ft (32,5 m²).

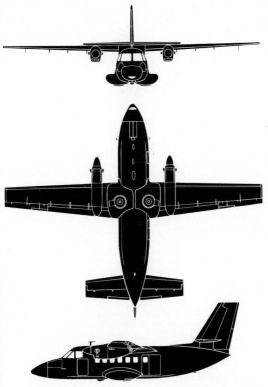

LOCKHEED C-130H HERCULES

Country of Origin: USA.

Type: Medium- to long-range military transport.

Power Plant: Four 4,050 eshp Allison T56-A-7A turbo-props.

Performance: Max. speed, 384 mph (618 km/h); max. cruise, 368 mph (592 km/h); econ. cruise, 340 mph (547 km/h); range (with max. payload and 5% plus 30 min reserves), 2,450 mls (3 943 km); max. range, 4,770 mls (7 675 km); initial climb, 1,900 ft/min (9,65 m/sec).

Weights: Empty equipped, 72,892 lb (33 063 kg); max. normal take-off, 155,000 lb (70 310 kg); max. overload, 175,000 lb (79 380 kg).

Accommodation: Flight crew of four and max. of 92 fully-equipped troops, 64 paratroops, or 74 casualty stretchers and two medical attendants. As a cargo carrier up to six pre-loaded freight pallets may be carried.

Status: The C-130H is the principal current production version of the Hercules which, in progressively developed forms, has been in continuous production since 1952, and at the beginning of 1973, when more than 1,200 Hercules had been ordered, production rate was three per month.

Notes: The C-130H, which was in process of delivery to Belgium, Italy and Iran at the beginning of 1973, is basically a C-130E with more powerful engines, and the Hercules C Mk. 1 (C-130K) serving with the RAF differs in having some UK-supplied instruments, avionics and other items.

LOCKHEED C-130H HERCULES

Dimensions: Span, 132 ft 7 in (40,41 m); length, 97 ft 9 in (29,78 m); height, 38 ft 3 in (11,66 m); wing area, 1,745 sq ft (162,12 m²).

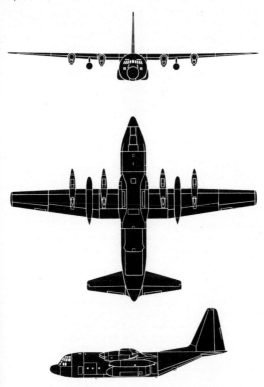

LOCKHEED C-5A GALAXY

Country of Origin: USA.

Type: Long-range military strategic transport.

Power Plant: Four 41,000 lb (18 600 kg) General Electric TF39-GE-1 turbofans.

Performance: Max. speed, 571 mph (919 km/h) at 25,000 ft (7 620 m); max. cruise at 525,000 lb (238 150 kg), 541 mph (871 km/h) at 30,000 ft (9 150 m); econ. cruise at 675,000 lb (306 175 kg), 537 mph (864 km/h) at 30,000 ft (9 150 m); range with max. fuel, 80,000-lb (36 287-kg) payload and reserves of 5% and 30 min, 6,500 mls (10 460 km), with max. payload and same reserves, 2,950 mls (4 745 km); initial climb at max. take-off, 2,300 ft/min (11,7 m/sec); service ceiling at 615,000 lb (278 950 kg), 34,000 ft (10 360 m).

Weights: Basic operational, 325,244 lb (147 528 kg); max. take-off, 764,500 lb (346 770 kg).

Accommodation: Basic flight crew of five plus relief crew and courier seating for 10. Seating for 75 troops on rear of upper deck, and provision for carrying 270 troops on lower deck. Typical freight loads include two M-60 tanks, an M-60 tank and two Iroquois helicopters, five M-113 personnel carriers, two Minutemen missiles on transporters, or 10 Pershing missiles with tow and launch vehicles.

Status: First of eight test and evaluation aircraft flown June 30, 1968, and first delivery to USAF made on December 17, 1969. Current orders for 81 C-5As scheduled for completion May 1973, production rate being two per month at the beginning of 1973.

Notes: USAF Military Airlift Command has four C-5A squadrons each with 16 aircraft.

142

LOCKHEED C-5A GALAXY

Dimensions: Span, 222 ft 8½ in (67,88 m); length, 247 ft 10 in (75,54 m); height, 65 ft 1½ in (19,85 m); wing area, 6,200 sq ft (576 m²).

143

LOCKHEED P-3C ORION

Country of Origin: USA.

Type: Long-range maritime patrol aircraft.

Power Plant: Four 4,910 eshp Allison T56-A-14W turbo-props.

Performance: Max. speed at 105,000 lb (47 625 kg), 437 mph (703 km/h) at 15,000 ft (4 570 m); normal cruise, 397 mph (639 km/h) at 25,000 ft (7 620 ml); patrol speed, 230 mph (370 km/h) at 1,500 ft (457 m); loiter endurance (all engines) at 1,500 ft (457 ml), 12·3 hours, (two engines), 17 hrs; max. mission radius, 2,530 mls (4 075 km), with 3 hrs on station at 1,500 ft (457 m), 1,933 mls (3 110 km); initial climb, 2,880 ft/min (14,6 m/sec); service ceiling, 28,300 ft (8 625 m).

Weights: Empty, 62,000 lb (28 123 kg); normal max. take-off, 133,500 lb (60 558 kg); max. overload, 142,000 lb (64 410 kg).

Accommodation: Normal flight crew of 10 of which five housed in tactical compartment. Up to 50 combat troops and up to 4,000 lb (1 814 kg) of equipment may be carried in the emergency trooping role.

Armament: Weapons bay can house two Mk 101 depth bombs and four Mk 43, 44 or 46 torpedoes, or eight Mk 54 bombs. External ordnance load of up to 13,713 lb (6 220 kg).

Status: YP-3C prototype flown October 8, 1968, with P-3C production deliveries commencing to US Navy mid-1969.

Notes: The P-3C differs from the P-3A and -3B primarily in having more advanced sensor equipment. Twelve P-3As have been modified as EP-3Es for the electronic reconnaissance role, others have been adapted for the weather reconnaissance role as WP-3As, and a specially-equipped version, the RP-3D, is being used to map the earth's magnetic field.

LOCKHEED P-3C ORION

Dimensions: Span, 99 ft 8 in (30,37 m); length, 116 ft 10 in (35,61 m); height, 33 ft 8½ in (10,29 m); wing area, 1,300 sq ft (120,77 m²).

LOCKHEED F-104S STARFIGHTER

Country of Origin: USA.

Type: Single-seat interceptor and strike fighter.

Power Plant: One 11,870 lb (5 385 kg) dry and 17,900 lb (8 120 kg) reheat General Electric J79-GE-19 turbojet.

Performance: Max. speed, 910 mph (1 470 km/h) or Mach 1·2 at sea level, 1,450 mph (2 335 km/h) or Mach 2·2 at 36,000 ft (10 970 m); max. cruise, 610 mph (980 km/h) at 36,000 ft (10 970 m); tactical radius with two 162 Imp gal (736 l) and two 100 Imp gal (455 l) drop tanks, 740–775 mls (1 190–1 245 km); ferry range, 1,815 mls (2 920 km); initial climb, 50,000 plus ft/min (254 plus m/sec).

Weights: Empty, 14,573 lb (6 610 kg); loaded (clean), 21,307 lb (9 665 kg); max. take-off, 31,000 lb (14 060 kg).

Armament: One 20-mm M-61 rotary cannon, two AIM-7 Sparrow III and two AIM-9 Sidewinder AAMs.

Status: First of two Lockheed-built F-104S prototypes flown December 1966, and first Fiat-built production F-104S flown December 30, 1968. Production of 205 for Italian Air Force continuing at rate of two–three per month at beginning of 1973 with 100th delivered in January 1973 and deliveries scheduled for completion in 1976.

Notes: Derivative of the F-104G (see 1966 edition) optimised for all-weather intercept role. Features uprated engine with redesigned afterburner. Nine external stores attachment points.

LOCKHEED F-104S STARFIGHTER

Dimensions: Span, 21 ft 11 in (6,68 m); length, 54 ft 9 in (16,69 m); height, 13 ft 6 in (4,11 m); wing area, 196·1 sq ft (18,22 m²).

LOCKHEED L-1011-1 TRISTAR

Country of Origin: USA.

Type: Short- to medium-range commercial transport.

Power Plant: Three 42,000 lb (19 050 kg) Rolls-Royce RB.211-22B turbofans.

Performance: (Estimated) Max. cruise at max. take-off weight, 590 mph (950 km/h) at 35,000 ft (10 670 m); econ. cruise, 540 mph (870 km/h) at 35,000 ft (10 670 m); range with max. fuel and 40,000 lb (18 145 kg) payload, 4,467 mls (7 189 km); range with max. payload comprising 256 passengers and 5,000 lb (2 270 kg) cargo, 2,878 mls (4 629 km); initial climb, 2,800 ft/min (14,2 m/sec); service ceiling, 35,000 ft (10 670 m).

Weights: Empty, 218,999 lb (99 336 kg); operational empty, 234,275 lb (106 265 kg); max. take-off, 430,000 lb (195 045 kg).

Accommodation: Basic flight crew of three–four. Typical passenger configuration provides 256 seats in a ratio of 20% first class and 80% coach class. An all-economy configuration provides for 345 passengers, while up to 400 may be accommodated in a high-density configuration.

Status: First L-1011-1 flown November 16, 1970, with first deliveries (to Eastern) following in April 1972. By the end of January 1973 orders and "second buy" options totalled 199 aircraft.

Notes: The Model 193 (L-1011) TriStar is the first aircraft to employ the RB.211 engine, and at the beginning of 1973 various long-range versions of the basic design were under study.

LOCKHEED L-1011-1 TRISTAR

Dimensions: Span, 155 ft 4 in (47,34 m); length, 177 ft 8½ in (54,16 m); height, 55 ft 4 in (16,87 m); wing area, 3,755 sq ft (348,85 m²).

LOCKHEED S-3A VIKING

Country of Origin: USA.

Type: Four-seat shipboard anti-submarine aircraft.

Power Plant: Two 9,000 lb (4 082 kg) General Electric TF34-GE-2 turbofans.

Performance: (Estimated) Max. speed, 495 mph (797 km/h); max. cruise, 403 mph (649 km/h); typical loiter speed, 184 mph (257 km/h); max. ferry range, 3,500 mls (5 630 km) plus; service ceiling, 35,000 ft (10 670 m).

Weights: (Estimated) Empty equipped, 26,600 lb (12 065 kg); normal take-off, 42,000 lb (19 050 kg); max. take-off, 47,000 lb (21 320 kg).

Accommodation: Pilot and co-pilot side by side on flight deck, with tactical co-ordinator and sensor operator in aft cabin. All four crew members provided with zero-zero ejection seats.

Armament: Various combinations of torpedoes, depth charges, bombs and ASMs in internal weapons bay and on underwing pylons.

Status: First of eight development and evaluation aircraft commenced its test programme on January 21, 1972, and three more had flown by the beginning of 1973, the remaining four being scheduled to fly early in 1973. Current US Navy planning calls for acquisition of 191 production aircraft during fiscal years 1972–75.

Notes: Intended as a successor to the Grumman S-2 Tracker in US Navy service, Lockheed's shipboard turbofan-powered ASW aircraft was selected for development mid-1969 after competitive evaluation of a number of proposals, and is scheduled to enter fleet service early in 1974.

LOCKHEED S-3A VIKING

Dimensions: Span, 68 ft 8 in (20,93 m); length, 53 ft 4 in (16,26 m); height, 22 ft 9 in (6,93 m); wing area, 598 sq ft (55,56 m²).

McDONNELL DOUGLAS DC-9 SERIES 30

Country of Origin: USA.
Type: Short-range commercial transport.
Power Plant: Two 14,000 lb (6 350 kg) Pratt & Whitney JT8D-7 turbofans.
Performance: Max. cruise, 565 mph (909 km/h) at 25,000 ft (7 620 m); econ. cruise, 534 mph (860 km/h) at 33,000 ft (10 058 m); long-range cruise, 494 mph (796 km/h) at 35,000 ft (10 668 m); range (with reserves for 230 mls/370 km and 60 min hold) at econ. cruise, 1,484 mls (2 388 km), at long-range cruise, 1,725 mls (2 775 km).
Weights: Empty, 52,935 lb (24 011 kg); max. take-off, 98,000 lb (44 450 kg).
Accommodation: Flight crew of two—three and normal seating for up to 105 passengers or (with limited facilities) 115 passengers.
Status: The Series 30 was first flown on August 1, 1966, and the first delivery (to Eastern) was made on January 27, 1967. This version of the DC-9 has since been built in substantially larger numbers than other models.
Notes: The DC-9 was first flown on February 25, 1965, and production versions include the initial Series 10, the Series 20 (see 1969 edition) retaining the short fuselage of the Series 10 which was married to the longer-span wings of the Series 30, and the Series 40 (see 1972 edition) embodying a further fuselage stretch. The C-9A and C-9B are respectively aeromedical and logistic support transport versions of the Series 30 for the USAF and US Navy, 21 of the former and eight of the latter having been delivered.

McDONNELL DOUGLAS DC-9 SERIES 30

Dimensions: Span, 93 ft 5 in (28,47 m); length, 119 ft 3½ in (36,37 m); height, 27 ft 6 in (8,38 m); wing area, 1,000·7 sq ft (92,97 m²).

McDONNELL DOUGLAS DC-10 SERIES 30

Country of Origin: USA.

Type: Medium-range commercial transport.

Power Plant: Three 49,000 lb (22 226 kg) General Electric CF6-50A turbofans.

Performance: Max. cruise (at 520,000 lb/235 868 kg), 570 mph (917 km/h) at 31,000 ft (9 450 m); long-range cruise, 554 mph (891 km/h) at 31,000 ft (9 450 m); max. fuel range (with 230 mls/370 km reserves), 6,909 mls (11 118 km); max. payload range, 4,272 mls (6 875 km); max. climb rate, 2,320 ft/min (11,78 m/sec); service ceiling (at 540,000 lb/244 940 kg), 32,700 ft (9 965 m).

Weights: Basic operating, 253,087 lb (119 334 kg); max. take-off, 555,000 lb (251 745 kg).

Accommodation: Flight crew of three plus provision on flight deck for two supernumerary crew. Typical mixed-class accommodation for 225–270 passengers. Max. authorised passenger accommodation, 380 (plus crew of 11).

Status: First DC-10 (Series 10) flown August 29, 1970, with first Series 30 (46th DC-10 built) flying June 21, 1972, being preceded on February 28, 1972, by first Series 40. Orders and options totalled 221 by January 1973.

Notes: The DC-10 Series 30 and 40 have identical fuselages to the DC-10 Series 10 (see 1972 edition), but whereas the last-mentioned version is a domestic model, the Series 30 and 40 are intercontinental models, and differ in power plant, weight and wing details, and in the use of three main undercarriage units, the third being mounted on the fuselage centreline.

McDONALD DOUGLAS DC-10 SERIES 30

Dimensions: Span, 161 ft 4 in (49,17 m); length, 181 ft 4¾ in (55,29 m); height, 58 ft 0 in (17,68 m); wing area, 3,921·4 sq ft (364,3 m²).

McDONNELL DOUGLAS A-4N SKYHAWK II

Country of Origin: USA.

Type: Single-seat light attack bomber.

Power Plant: One 11,200 lb (5 080 kg) Pratt & Whitney J52-P-408A turbojet.

Performance: Max. speed without external stores, 685 mph (1 102 km/h) or Mach 0·9 at sea level, 640 mph (1 030 km/h) at 25,000 ft (7 620 m), in high drag configuration, 625 mph (1 080 km/h) or Mach 0·82 at sea level, 605 mph (973 km/h) or Mach 0·84 at 30,000 ft (9 145 m); combat radius on internal fuel for hi-lo-lo-hi mission profile with 4,000 lb (1 814 kg) of external stores, 340 mls (547 km); initial climb, 15,850 ft/min (80,5 m/sec), at 23,000 lb (10 433 kg), 8,440 ft/min (42,7 m/sec).

Weights: Empty, 10,600 lb (4 808 kg); max. take-off, 24,500 lb (11 113 kg).

Armament: Two 30-mm DEFA cannon and external weapons loads up to 8,200 lb (3 720 kg) on wing and fuselage hardpoints.

Status: First A-4N flown June 12, 1972, with first production deliveries (to Israel) scheduled to have commenced November 1972.

Notes: The A-4N employs essentially the same power plant and airframe as the A-4M (see 1972 edition), both models being referred to as the Skyhawk II. The A-4N embodies some of the features originally developed for the A-4H (e.g., twin 30-mm cannon) but has a new nav/attack system (similar to that of the A-7D and -7E Corsair) and a revised cockpit layout.

McDONNELL DOUGLAS A-4N SKYHAWK II

Dimensions: Span, 27 ft 6 in (8,38 m); length, 40 ft 3¼ in (12,27 m); height, 15 ft 0 in (4,57 m); wing area, 260 sq ft (24,16 m²).

McDONNELL DOUGLAS F-4E
PHANTOM II

Country of Origin: USA.

Type: Two-seat tactical strike fighter.

Power Plant: Two 11,870 lb (5 385 kg) dry and 17,900 lb (8 120 kg) reheat General Electric J79-GE-17 turbojets.

Performance: Max. speed without external stores, 910 mph (1 464 km/h) or Mach 1·2 at 1,000 ft (305 m), 1,500 mph (2 414 km/h) or Mach 2·27 at 40,000 ft (12 190 m); tactical radius (with four Sparrow III and four Sidewinder AAMs), 140 mls (225 km), (plus one 500 Imp gal/2 273 l auxiliary tank), 196 mls (315 km), (hi-lo-hi mission profile with four 1,000-lb/453,6-kg bombs, four AAMs, and one 500 Imp gal/2 273 l and two 308 Imp gal/1 400 l tanks), 656 mls (1 056 km); max. ferry range, 2,300 mls (3 700 km) at 575 mph (925 km/h) at 40,000 ft (12 190 m).

Weights: Empty equipped, 30,425 lb (13 801 kg); loaded (with four Sparrow IIIs), 51,810 lb (21 500 kg), (plus four Sidewinders and max. external fuel), 58,000 lb (26 308 kg); max. overload, 60,630 lb (27 502 kg).

Armament: One 20-mm M-61A1 rotary cannon and (intercept) four or six AIM-7E Sparrow IIIB plus four AIM-9D Sidewinder AAMs, or (attack) up to 16,000 lb (7 257 kg) of external stores.

Status: First F-4E flown June 30, 1967, and production continuing at beginning of 1973 when some 4,900 Phantoms of all versions had been delivered.

Notes: Current production models of the Phantom in addition to the F-4E are the RF-4E (see 1972 edition), the F-4EJ for Japan and the F-4F for Federal Germany.

158

McDONNELL DOUGLAS F-4E PHANTOM II

Dimensions: Span, 38 ft 4¾ in (11,70 m); length, 62 ft 10½ in (19,20 m); height, 16 ft 3⅓ in (4,96 m); wing area, 530 sq ft (49,2 m²).

McDONNELL DOUGLAS F-15 EAGLE

Country of Origin: USA.

Type: Single-seat air-superiority fighter.

Power Plant: Two (approx.) 19,000 lb (8 618 kg) dry and 27,000 lb (12 247 kg) reheat Pratt & Whitney F100-PW-101 turbofans.

Performance: Max. sustained speed (approx.), 1,520 mph (2 446 km/h) or Mach 2·3 above 36,000 ft (10 975 m); max. short-period dash speed, 1,650 mph (2 655 km/h) or Mach 2·5; max. low-altitude speed (approx.), 915 mph (1 470 km/h) or Mach 1·2 at 1,000 ft (3 05 m).

Weights: Approx. max. loaded (air superiority mission), 40,000 lb (18 144 kg); max. take-off, 56,000 lb (25 400 kg).

Armament: One 20-mm M-61A-1 rotary cannon (eventually to be replaced by a 25-mm Philco-Ford GAU-7/A rotary cannon) and mix of four Raytheon AIM-7F Sparrow and four Raytheon AIM-9L Sidewinder AAMs.

Status: First of 20 development and test Eagles flown on July 27, 1972, with second and third following on September 26 and November 4, 1972, respectively. Eight of these 20 aircraft are to be used for service evaluation and 12 for the contractor's test programme. The Eagle is expected to enter the USAF inventory during 1975 and current planning calls for the purchase of 729 fighters of this type during Fiscal Years 1974–77.

Notes: Intended to provide the USAF with its principal air superiority capability during the period 1975–85, the Eagle is allegedly capable of climbing vertically at supersonic speed and of accelerating from subsonic cruise to speed of the order of Mach 1·5 within less than one minute.

160

McDONNELL DOUGLAS F-15 EAGLE

Dimensions: Span, 42 ft 9½ in (13,04 m); length, 63 ft 9½ in (19,44 m); height, 18 ft 7¼ in (5,67 m).

MIKOYAN MIG-21MF (FISHBED-J)

Country of Origin: USSR.

Type: Single-seat multi-purpose fighter.

Power Plant: One 11,244 lb (5 100 kg) dry and 14,550 lb (6 600 kg) Tumansky R-11 turbojet.

Performance: Max. speed, 808 mph (1 300 km/h) or Mach 1·06 at 1,000 ft (305 m), 1,386 mph (2 230 km/h) or Mach 2·1 above 36,090 ft (11 000 m); range on internal fuel, 683 mls (1 100 km); ferry range with max. external fuel, 1,118 mls (1 800 km); service ceiling, 59,055 ft (18 000 m).

Weights: Normal take-off (with four K-13 AAMs), 18,078 lb (8 200 kg), (with two K-13s and two 110 Imp gal/500 l drop tanks), 19,731 lb (8950 kg); max. take-off (with two K-13s and three drop tanks), 20,723 lb (9 400 kg).

Armament: Two 23-mm cannon with 100 rpg in fuselage and up to four K-13 (Atoll) AAMs on wing pylons for intercept role. Four 550-lb (250-kg) bombs or four 220-mm or 325-mm ASMs.

Status: The MiG-21MF is a progressive development of the MiG-21PFM (*Fishbed-D*), and entered service with the Soviet Air Forces in the late 'sixties. Manufactured in parallel is a reconnaissance version (*Fishbed-H*), and licence manufacture of the MiG-21PF (early *Fishbed-D*) is undertaken by HAL in India.

Notes: The MiG-21MF is equipped with a boundary layer blowing system known as SPS. The *Fishbed-C* (MiG-21F) and *-E* are clear-weather interceptors, and the reconnaissance *Fishbed-H* features wingtip ECM fairings.

MIKOYAN MIG-21MF (FISHBED-J)

Dimensions: Span, 23 ft $5\frac{1}{2}$ in (7,15 m); length (including probe), 51 ft $8\frac{1}{2}$ in (15,76 m), (without probe), 44 ft 2 in (13,46 m); wing area, 247·57 sq ft (23 m²).

MIKOYAN MIG-23 (FLOGGER)

Country of Origin: USSR.

Type: Single-seat interceptor fighter.

Power Plant: One (approx.) 28,000 lb (12 700 kg) reheat turbojet.

Performance: (Estimated) Max. speed, 865 mph (1 390 km/h) or Mach 1·2 at sea level, 1,520 mph (2 446 km/h) or Mach 2·3 at 39,370 ft (12 000 m), in high-drag configuration (e.g., two AAMs of advanced Anab type on fuselage stations and two AAMs on wing root stations), 1,120 mph (1 800 km/h) or Mach 1·7 at 39,370 ft (12 000 m); combat radius (with twin drop tanks on fuselage stations), 700 mls (1 126 km/h); service ceiling, 50,000 ft (15 250 m).

Weights: (Estimated) Normal take-off (with two AAMs), 30,000 lb (13 608 kg).

Armament: Two 23-mm or 30-mm cannon and up to four radar-guided AAMs on two fuselage and two wing root stations or mix of two infra-red ho'ming and two radar guided AAMs.

Status: Prototypes believed flown 1967 with production commencing early 1971.

Notes: The MiG-23 (this designation previously being attributed to the fixed-geometry fighter now known to be the MiG-25) is a variable-geometry fighter optimised for the air superiority role. According to US intelligence sources, the MiG-23 was in limited operational service with the Soviet Air Forces at the beginning of 1973 and its avionics are comparable with those of the F-4J Phantom.

164

MIKOYAN MIG-23 (FLOGGER)

Dimensions: (Estimated) Span (minimum sweep), 48 ft 0 in (14,63 m), (maximum sweep), 24 ft 0 in (7,31 m); length (including probe), 60 ft 0 in (18,29 m).

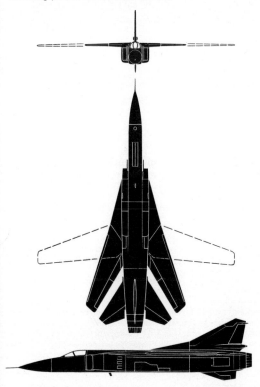

MIKOYAN MIG-25 (FOXBAT)

Country of Origin: USSR.
Type: Single-seat interceptor and reconnaissance fighter.
Power Plant: Two (approx.) 24,250 lb (11 000 kg) reheat Tumansky turbojets.
Performance: (Estimated) Max. short-period dash speed, 2,100 mph (3 380 km/h) or Mach 3·2 at 39,370 ft (12 000 m); max. sustained speed, 1,780 mph (2 865 km/h) or Mach 2·7 at 39,370 ft (12 000 m), 975 mph (1 570 km/h) or Mach 1·3 at 4,920 ft (1 500 m); normal combat radius, 700 mls (1 125 km); time to 36,000 ft (10 970 m), 2·5 min.
Weights: (Estimated) Empty equipped, 34,000 lb (15 420 kg); normal loaded, 50,000–55,000 lb (22 680–24 950 kg); max. take-off, 64,200 lb (29 120 kg).
Armament: Four wing stations for radar homing AAMs for the intercept role. Internal bay in the fore-part of each air intake trunk, forward of the wheel well capable of housing reconnaissance equipment in place of 23-mm or 30-mm canon mounted by interceptor versions.
Status: Believed flown in prototype form 1963–64 with service deliveries following from 1970–71.
Notes: The MiG-25 multi-purpose fighter has established a number of FAI-recognised records since 1965 under the designation Ye-266. On October 5, 1967, the Ye-266 established a record of 1,852·61 mph (2 981,5 km/h), or Mach 2·8, over a 310-mile (500-km) closed circuit, following this on October 27 with a speed of 1,841·81 mph (2 920,67 km/h), or Mach 2·7, over a 621-mile (1 000-km) circuit. The MiG-25 (originally thought to be designated MiG-23— see pages 164–165) allegedly possesses an operational ceiling of 80,000 ft (24 385 m).

MIKOYAN MIG-25 (FOXBAT)

Dimensions: (Estimated) Span, 41 ft 0 in (12,5 m); length, 70 ft 0 in (21,33 m).

MITSUBISHI XT-2

Country of Origin: Japan.

Type: Tandem two-seat advanced trainer.

Power Plant: Two 4,600 lb (2 086 kg) dry and 6,950 lb (3 150 kg) reheat Rolls-Royce Turboméca RB.172-T.260 Adour turbofans.

Performance: (Estimated) Max. speed, 1,056 mph (1 700 km/h) or Mach 1·6 at 40,000 ft (12 190 m); max. ferry range, 1,600 mls (2 575 km); service ceiling, 50,000 ft.

Weights: (Estimated) Normal take-off, 21,000 lb (9 525 kg).

Armament: Provision for one 20-mm rotary cannon internally and various external ordnance loads on fuselage, underwing, and wingtip stations.

Status: First of two flying prototypes was flown on July 20, 1971, and four had been flown by the beginning of 1973. Current plans call for deliveries of 59 production T-2A trainers during the current five-year defence programme (1972–75).

Notes: Japan's first indigenous supersonic aircraft, the T-2A trainer is intended to enter the inventory of the Air Self-Defence Force in 1974. The basic design is also intended to fulfil operational roles, and the ASDF is to receive 68 examples of a close-support fighter version, the F-1, these entering the inventory from 1975 onwards. A single-seater, the F-1 will carry a 20-mm rotary cannon and eight 500-lb (227-kg) bombs, or 12 500-lb (227-kg) bombs in overload condition. Max. take-off weight will be 30,865 lb (14 000 kg). The first ASDF training squadron to receive the T-2A is scheduled to be formed during 1975, F-86F Sabres and T-33As currently used for advanced training being progressively withdrawn.

MITSUBISHI XT-2

Dimensions: Span, 25 ft 11 in (7,90 m); length, 58 ft 4¾ in (17,80 m); height, 14 ft 9¼ in (4,50 m); wing area, 228·2 sq ft (21,2 m²).

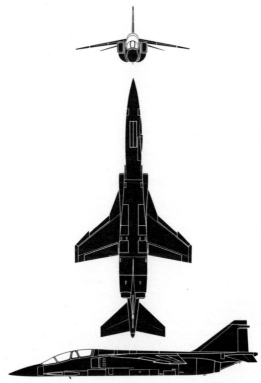

NORTH AMERICAN ROCKWELL
AERO COMMANDER 112

Country of Origin: USA.

Type: Light cabin monoplane.

Power Plant: One 200 hp Avco Lycoming IO-360-C1D6 four-cylinder horizontally-opposed engine.

Performance: Max. speed, 175 mph (281 km/h) at sea level; cruise at 75% power at optimum altitude, 165 mph (265 km/h); range at 75% power (no reserves), 960 mls (1 545 km); optimum range, 1,130 mls (1 818 km); initial climb, 1,000 ft/min (5,08 m/sec); service ceiling, 17,000 ft (5 182 m).

Weights: Empty, 1,530 lb (694 kg); max. take-off, 2,550 lb (1 157 kg).

Accommodation: Pilot and three passengers seated in pairs with individual seats forward and bench seat aft.

Status: The first of five prototypes was flown on December 4, 1970, and customer deliveries were scheduled to commence late 1972.

Notes: The development programme of the Aero Commander 112 has been somewhat protracted owing to modifications to the tail assembly necessitated by the loss of a prototype during high-speed diving trials, FAA certification being obtained during the course of 1972. The parallel Aero Commander 111A (see 1972 edition) features a fixed undercarriage and a 180 hp Lycoming O-360-A1G6 engine driving a constant-speed airscrew. A twin-engined version of the basic design is planned, and six-seat versions of both the Aero Commander 111A and 112 are projected.

NORTH AMERICAN ROCKWELL
AERO COMMANDER 112

Dimensions: Span, 32 ft 9 in (9,98 m); length, 24 ft 11 in (7,59 m); height, 8 ft 5 in (2,51 m); wing area, 152 sq ft (14,12 m²).

NORTH AMERICAN ROCKWELL
AERO COMMANDER 685

Country of Origin: USA.

Type: Light business executive transport.

Power Plant: Two 435 hp Teledyne Continental GTSIO-520F six-cylinder horizontally-opposed engines.

Performance: Max. speed, 290 mph (467 km/h); max. cruise, 258 mph (415 km/h); cruise at 65% power, 251 mph (404 km/h) at 25,000 ft (7 620 m), 230 mph (370 km/h) at 15,000 ft (4 572 m); range at 65% power (pilot and four passengers), 823 mls (1 325 km) at 25,000 ft (7 620 m), (pilot and seven passengers), 444 mls (714 km) at 20,000 ft (6 096 m); initial climb, 1,490 ft/min (7,57 m/sec).

Weights: Empty equipped, 6,021 lb (2 731 kg); max. take-off, 9,000 lb (4 082 kg).

Accommodation: Standard seating for eight persons (including pilot) in fully pressurised cabin, with side-by-side seats on flight deck, two rearward-facing single seats, a three-place forward-facing bench seat, and a single side-facing seat.

Status: Flown for the first time in 1971 with production deliveries commencing April 1972.

Notes: The Aero Commander 685 is basically the Turbo Commander 690 with the 717 eshp AiResearch TPE-331-5-251K turboprops replaced by piston engines. The Aero Commander 685 is manufactured in parallel with the smaller and lower-powered Shrike Commander and the higher-performance Turbo Commander, all three aircraft being of similar construction and configuration.

NORTH AMERICAN ROCKWELL
AERO COMMANDER 685

Dimensions: Span, 46 ft 6⅔ in (14,23 m); length, 42 ft 11¼ in (13,10 m); height, 14 ft 11⅓ in (4,56 m); wing area, 266 sq ft (24,7 m²).

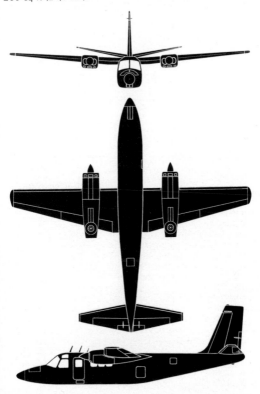

NORTH AMERICAN ROCKWELL SABRE 75A

Country of Origin: USA.

Type: Light business executive transport.

Power Plant: Two 4,315 lb (1 961 kg) General Electric CF700-20-2 turbofans.

Performance: Max. cruise (at 21,370 lb/9 693 kg), 555 mph (893 km/h); long-range cruise, 462 mph (743 km/h); range (four passengers and 45 min reserves), 1,820 mls (2 930 km), (10 passengers and 45 min reserves), 1,695 mls (2 730 km); initial climb (at 21,370 lb/9 693 kg), 4,875 ft/min (24,76 m/sec).

Weights: Empty equipped, 12,900 lb (5 851 kg); max. take-off, 23,100 lb (10 478 kg).

Accommodation: Normal flight crew of two and various arrangements for six to 10 passengers.

Status: Prototype Sabre 75A flown initially on October 18, 1972, with certification anticipated for early 1973.

Notes: The Sabre 75A is a variant of the Sabre 75 (see 1972 edition) which it replaces and from which it differs primarily in having turbofans in place of JT12A-8 turbojets, cascade-type thrust reversers, an increase in maximum fuel capacity, new high-energy disc brakes with an anti-skid system, and a new integral air-stair door. The Sabre 75A employs the same wings as those of the Sabre Commander 40A and the Sabreliner Series 60 (see 1968 edition) but has an entirely new fuselage of deeper section. The Sabreliner series has been in continuous production for 15 years.

NORTH AMERICAN ROCKWELL SABRE 75A

Dimensions: Span, 44 ft 3⅔ in (13,50 m); length, 47 ft 0 in (14,32 m); height, 17 ft 3 in (5,26 m); wing area, 342·05 sq ft (31,78 m²).

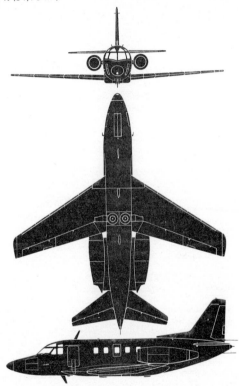

NORTHROP F-5E TIGER II

Country of Origin: USA.
Type: Single-seat air-superiority fighter.
Power Plant: Two 3,500 lb (1 588 kg) dry and 5,000 lb (2 268 kg) reheat General Electric J85-GE-21 turbojets.
Performance: Max. speed (at 13,220 lb/5 997 kg), 1056 mph (1 700 km/h) or Mach 1·6 at 36,090 ft (11 000 m), 760 mph (1 223 km/h) or Mach 1·0 at sea level, (with wing-tip missiles), 990 mph (1 594 km/h) or Mach 1·5 at 36,090 ft (11 000 m); combat radius (internal fuel), 173 mls (278 km), (with 229 Imp gal/1 041 I drop tank), 426 mls (686 km), initial climb (at 13,220 lb/5 997 kg), 31,600 ft/min (160,53 m/sec); combat ceiling, 53,500 ft (16 305 m).
Weights: Take-off (wingtip launching rail configuration), 15,400 lb (6 985 kg); max. take-off, 24,083 lb (10 924 kg).
Armament: Two 20-mm M-39 cannon with 280 rpg and two wingtip-mounted AIM-9 Sidewinder AAMs. Up to 7,000 lb (3 175 kg) of ordnance (for attack role) on five external hardpoints.
Status: First F-5E flown August 11, 1972, and first deliveries scheduled for February 1973. Production rate of 10 per month anticipated from early 1975.
Notes: A more powerful derivative of the F-5A (see 1970 edition) optimised for the air-superiority role, the F-5E won the USAF's International Fighter Aircraft (IFA) contest in November 1970, and the USAF has options on the production of up to 325 for supply under the Military Assistance Programme to South Korea, South Vietnam, Taiwan, Thailand and Jordan. Orders for the F-5E have also been placed by Iran, Saudi Arabia and Malaysia.

NORTHROP F-5E TIGER II

Dimensions: Span, 26 ft 8½ in (8,14 m); length, 48 ft 2½ in (14,69 m); height, 13 ft 4 in (4,06 m); wing area, 186·2 sq ft (17,29 m²).

PANAVIA MRCA

Country of Origin: International consortium.

Type: Two-seat multi-purpose fighter.

Power Plant: Two 8,500 lb (3 855 kg) dry and 14,500 lb (6 577 kg) reheat Turbo-Union RB.199-34R turbofans.

Performance: Max. speed, 1,320+ mph (2 125+ km/h) or Mach 2·0+ above 36,000 ft (10 970 m), approx. 910 mph (1 465 km/h) at low altitude; combat endurance on internal fuel, approx. 70–80 min.

Weights: Empty equipped, 22,000–23,000 lb (9 980–10 430 kg); loaded, 38,000–40,000 lb (17 240–18 145 kg).

Armament: Two 27-mm Mauser cannon internally and various loads on three fuselage and four wing pylons.

Status: First of six prototypes scheduled to fly late 1973 with remainder together with three pre-production aircraft to have joined the development programme by September 1975. Four of these development aeroplanes to be built in the UK, three in Federal Germany and two in Italy. Six further pre-production aircraft to be used in test programme and service deliveries to commence 1977–78 with current planning calling for 322 aircraft for the Federal German *Luftwaffe* and *Marineflieger*, some 385 for the RAF (of which approximately 165 will be optimised for the intercept role with the remainder being for interdiction strike), and about 100 for Italy's *Aeronautica Militare*.

Notes: The MRCA (multi-role combat aircraft) is being developed by Panavia Aircraft GmbH, a multi-national European industrial company formed by the British Aircraft Corporation, Messerschmitt-Bölkow-Blohm and Fiat.

PANAVIA MRCA

Dimensions: No details available for publication.

PARTENAVIA P.68 VICTOR

Country of Origin: Italy.

Type: Light utility transport.

Power Plant: Two 200 hp Lycoming IO-360-A1B four-cylinder horizontally-opposed engines.

Performance: Max. speed, 201 mph (324 km/h) at sea level; cruise at 75% power, 196 mph (316 km/h) at 8,200 ft (2 500 m), at 65% power, 194 mph (313 km/h) at 11,810 ft (3 600 m); range at 65% power with 30 min reserves at 55% power, 932 mls (1 500 km); initial climb, 1,850 ft/min (9,4 m/sec); service ceiling, 26,575 ft (8 100 m).

Weights: Empty, 2,216 lb (1 005 kg); max. take-off, 3,878 lb (1 760 kg).

Accommodation: Seating for pilot and five passengers in three pairs of side-by-side seats.

Status: First prototype flown on May 25, 1970, 10 pre-production aircraft completed during 1972, and production to attain three per month during 1973. The P.68 is being offered with either 180 or 200 hp engines and either fixed or retractable undercarriage.

Notes: Placing emphasis on simplicity and ease of maintenance and operation, the P.68 possesses short-field capability and has been designed to fulfil such roles as air taxi, light utility transport, and ambulance. A slightly stretched Victor (the 13th aircraft built) accommodating eight persons is under development as is also a STOL version with leading-edge slats and double-slotted flaps. Modular design will permit manufacture of several variants without major changes in production facilities.

PARTENAVIA P.68 VICTOR

Dimensions: Span, 39 ft 4½ in (12,00 m); length, 29 ft 11 in (9,12 m); height, 10 ft 8 in (3,25 m); wing area, 200·2 sq ft (18,6 m²).

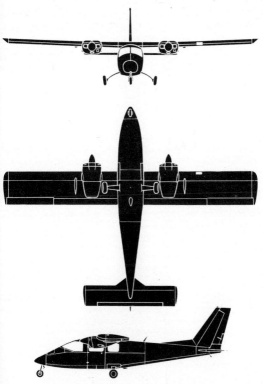

PARTENAVIA P.70 ALPHA

Country of Origin: Italy.

Type: Side-by-side two-seat primary trainer.

Power Plant: One 100 hp Rolls-Royce/Continental O-200-A four-cylinder horizontally-opposed engine.

Performance: Max. speed, 140 mph (225 km/h) at sea level; cruise at 75% power, 130 mph (209 km/h) at 7,000 ft (2 135 m); max. range, 547 mls (880 km); initial climb, 800 ft/min (4,06 m/sec); service ceiling, 13,125 ft (4 000 m).

Weights: Empty equipped, 1,035 lb (470 kg); max. take-off, 1,585 lb (720 kg).

Status: Prototype flown for first time on May 27, 1972, with production deliveries planned for 1974.

Notes: Emphasising sturdiness and simplicity, the Alpha makes extensive use of plastics for secondary structures and is the latest in a long series of light aircraft produced by Partenavia Costruzioni Aeronautiche of Naples. Intended primarily as an economical club trainer, the Alpha is proposed in a fully aerobatic version with a 130 hp Rolls-Royce/Continental O-240-A engine, and variants with 150, 180 and 200 hp engines are projected as is also a four-seat model which, if proceeded with, will supplant the high-wing P.66 Oscar in the Partenavia range. The Alpha is stressed for +6g to −3g limit loads, features an all-moving tailplane operated by push-pull rods, has fully duplicated flight controls, and has provision for instrumentation from basic VFR to complete IFR.

PARTENAVIA P.70 ALPHA

Dimensions: Span, 27 ft 10½ in (8,50 m); length, 23 ft 0 in (7,00 m); height, 9 ft 1½ in (2,78 m); wing area, 124·86 sq ft (11,60 m²).

PIPER PA-28-180
CHEROKEE CHALLENGER

Country of Origin: USA.

Type: Light cabin monoplane.

Power Plant: One 180 hp Avco Lycoming O-360-A3A four-cylinder horizontally-opposed engine.

Performance: Max. speed, 148 mph (238 km/h); range cruise, 141 mph (227 km/h) at 7,000 ft (2 134 m); range, 688 mls (1 107 km) at 141 mph (227 km/h) at 7,000 ft (2 134 m); initial climb, 725 ft/min (3,68 m/sec).

Weights: Empty equipped, 1,386 lb (628 kg); max. take-off, 2,450 lb (1 110 kg).

Accommodation: Four persons in pairs in enclosed cabin. Full dual controls and individual seats.

Status: The Cherokee Challenger was introduced late in 1972 as the successor to the Cherokee 180 in 1973 range.

Notes: The Cherokee Challenger differs from the Cherokee 180 in having increased wingspan, new wingtips, an enlarged cabin and a larger all-moving tailplane. The basic Cherokee has been in continuous production since 1960, and models in the 1973 range include the PA-28-235 Cherokee Charger with a 235 hp O-540-B4B5 engine, the PA-28-200 with a 200 hp IO-360-C1C and retractable undercarriage, the PA-28-140 Cherokee 140 Cruiser with a 150 hp O-320 with 2+2 seating, the similarly-powered Flite Liner two-seat trainer, and the PA-32-260 and PA-32-300 Cherokee Six with 260 hp O-540-E and 300 hp IO-540-K respectively and six seats.

184

PIPER PA-28-180 CHEROKEE CHALLENGER

Dimensions: Span, 32 ft 0 in (9,75 m); length, 24 ft 0 in (7,31 m); height 7 ft 9⅝ in (2,38 m); wing area, 170 sq ft (15,79 m²).

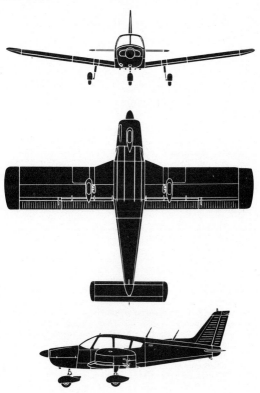

PIPER PA-31-350 NAVAJO CHIEFTAIN

Country of Origin: USA.

Type: Light business executive and utility transport.

Power Plant: Two 350 hp Avco Lycoming LTIO/TIO-540-J2BD six-cylinder horizontally-opposed engines.

Performance: Max. speed, 270 mph (435 km/h) at 15,000 ft (4 570 m); max. cruise, 260 mph (418 km/h) at 24,000 ft (7 315 m); econ. cruise, 232 mph (373 km/h) at 12,000 ft (3 658 m), 235 mph (378 km/h) at 24,000 ft (7 315 m); range with 45 min reserves, 925 mls (1 490 km) at 12,000 ft (3 658 m), 1,100 mls (1 770 km) at 24,000 ft (7 315 m); initial climb, 1,390 ft/min (7,0 m/sec).

Weights: Empty equipped, 3,991 lb (1 808 kg); max. take-off, 7,000 lb (3 171 kg).

Accommodation: Provision for up to five rows of paired seats, including two crew seats (or pilot plus passenger). Basic version has seating for pilot and seven passengers.

Status: The Navajo Chieftain is an addition to the 1973 range of PA-31 Navajo twin-engined aircraft, production deliveries having commenced late 1972.

Notes: A growth version of the PA-31 Turbo Navajo B (see 1972 edition), the Navajo Chieftain features a lengthened fuselage and higher-powered engines. The PA-31 Navajo was first flown on September 30, 1964, and the basic type has been in continuous production since 1967, current members of the Navajo range comprising the basic PA-31-300, the PA-31-310 Turbo Navajo and the PA-31P Pressurised Navajo.

PIPER PA-31-350 NAVAJO CHIEFTAIN

Dimensions: Span, 40 ft 8 in (12,40 m); length, 34 ft 8 in (10,60 m); height, 13 ft 0 in (3,96 m); wing area, 229 sq ft (21,3 m²).

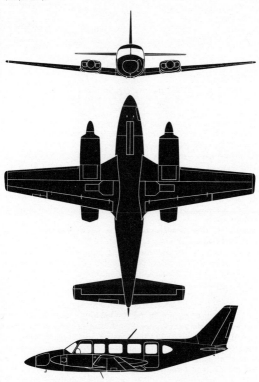

PIPER PA-36 PAWNEE BRAVE

Country of Origin: USA.

Type: Single-seat agricultural aircraft.

Power Plant: One 285 hp Teledyne Continental 6-285A six-cylinder horizontally-opposed engine.

Performance: Operating speed (min. application—sprayer), 135 mph (217 km/h), (max. application—sprayer), 90 mph (145 km/h).

Weights: Empty, 2,050 lb (930 kg); empty equipped (sprayer), 2,170 lb (984 kg); max. take-off (normal category), 3,900 lb (1 770 kg), (restricted category), 4,400 lb (1 996 kg).

Status: Under development since 1970, the PA-36 was being offered for delivery from late 1972.

Notes: Initially announced as the Pawnee II, the PA-36 Pawnee Brave shares only basic configuration with the earlier specialised Piper agricultural aircraft, the PA-25 Pawnee, being essentially a new design. The Pawnee Brave is being offered with two hopper sizes, one having 30 cu ft (0,85 m³) capacity and being intended primarily for spraying operations and the other having 38 cu ft (1,07 m³) capacity for dry chemicals. Safety provisions include the use of a totally isolated cockpit capsule which is sealed against the intrusion of toxic chemicals and positioned so that the pilot is well clear of primary structural members. The entire airframe is treated against damage through the corrosive effects of insecticides, and the fuel tanks are filled with reticulated polyurethane safety foam to reduce fire risk. Piper has built over 4,200 examples of the earlier PA-25 Pawnee.

PIPER PA-36 PAWNEE BRAVE

Dimensions: Span, 39 ft 0 in (11,89 m); length, 27 ft 4 in (8,33 m); wing area, 225 sq ft (20,9 m²).

PIPER PA-34 SENECA

Country of Origin: USA.

Type: Light business executive transport.

Power Plant: Two 200 hp Lycoming IO-360-A1A four-cylinder horizontally-opposed engines.

Performance: Max. speed, 195 mph (314 km/h); max. cruise, 186 mph (299 km/h) at 6,000 ft (1 830 m); cruise at 65% power, 184 mph (296 km/h) at 9,000 ft (2 743 m), at 55% power, 178 mph (286 km/h) at 13,300 ft (4 054 m); range at 75% power, 860 mls (1 385 km), at 65% power, 960 mls (1 545 km), at 55% power, 1,070 mls (1 722 km), at 45% power, 1,160 mls (1 866 km); initial climb, 1,360 ft/min (6,9 m/sec); ceiling, 20,000 ft (6 096 m).

Weights: Empty equipped, 2,599 lb (1 177 kg); max. take-off, 4,200 lb (1 903 kg).

Accommodation: Standard accommodation for six persons in individual seats with alternative arrangement for seven persons with a three-across centre seat.

Status: Announced in September 1971 with deliveries commencing late same year. Among changes incorporated in the 1973 model is a 200-lb (90,7-kg) increase in max. take-off weight.

Notes: The PA-34 Seneca is basically a twin-engined development of the single-engined PA-32 Cherokee Six, and is claimed by its manufacturer to be the lowest priced aircraft in its category. Emphasis has been placed on suitability for the twin-engined conversion training role.

PIPER PA-34 SENECA

Dimensions: Span, 38 ft 10¾ in (11,86 m); length, 28 ft 6 in (8,69 m); height, 9 ft 10¼ in (3,02 m); wing area, 206·5 sq ft (19,18 m²).

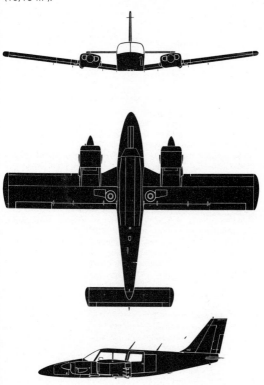

ROBIN HR 100/210 ROYALE

Country of Origin: France.

Type: Light cabin monoplane.

Power Plant: One 210 hp Teledyne Continental IO-360-D six-cylinder horizontally-opposed engine.

Performance: Max. speed, 177 mph (285 km/h) at sea level; cruise at 75% power, 158 mph (254 km/h) at sea level, 168 mph (270 km/h) at optimum altitude; range at 75% power with standard tankage, 850 mls (1 370 km), with auxiliary fuel, 1,687 mls (2 715 km); initial climb, 935 ft/min (4,73 m/sec); service ceiling, 16,400 ft (5 000 m).

Weights: Empty, 1,580 lb (716 kg); max. take-off, 2,780 lb (1 261 kg).

Accommodation: Seating for four persons in pairs under canopy which slides forward to provide access to all seats.

Status: First HR 100 prototype flown April 3, 1969, and first production HR 100/210 flown September 28, 1972.

Notes: The HR 100 was the first all-metal aircraft to be produced by Avions Pierre Robin, and is currently available as the HR 100/200 with a 200 hp Avco Lycoming IO-360-A1D6 and as the HR 100/210 described above. The HR 100/320, a prototype of which was flown on November 18, 1972, is the first Avions Robin type to feature a retractable undercarriage and in production form is to be powered by a 320 hp Teledyne Continental 6-320 Tiara six-cylinder engine. It is anticipated that the HR 100/210 will also be offered with a retractable undercarriage during the course of 1973.

ROBIN HR 100/210 ROYALE

Dimensions: Span, 29 ft 9½ in (9,08 m); length, 24 ft 5⅓ in (7,45 m); height, 7 ft 5 in (2,26 m); wing area, 163·61 sq ft (15,2 m²).

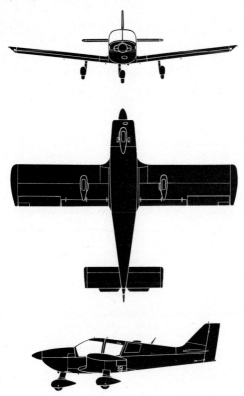

ROBIN HR 200 ACROBIN

Country of Origin: France.

Type: Fully-aerobatic light cabin monoplane.

Power Plant: One 100 hp Teledyne Continental O-200-A four-cylinder horizontally-opposed engine.

Performance: Max. speed, 143 mph (230 km/h) at sea level; cruise at 75% power, 124 mph (199 km/h) at sea level, 133 mph (214 km/h) at optimum altitude; range, 787 mls (1 266 km) at optimum altitude; initial climb, 669 ft/min (3,4 m/sec); service ceiling, 13,000 ft (3 962 m).

Weights: Empty equipped, 1,102 lb (500 kg); max. take-off, 1,680 lb (762 kg).

Accommodation: Pilot and passenger side-by-side on bench-type seat (with optional individual adjustable seats) beneath forward-sliding canopy.

Status: Prototype Acrobin flown July 30, 1971, with production deliveries scheduled to commence early 1973.

Notes: An all-metal two-seater stressed for aerobatics, the HR 200 Acrobin is an entirely new design despite its external resemblance to the HR 100 Royale (see pages 192–193). Intended specifically for flying clubs and schools, the Acrobin is to be offered with a 125 hp Avco Lycoming O-235 as an alternative to the O-200-A installed in the initial production model. Avions Pierre Robin anticipate delivering some 90 Acrobins during the course of 1973 with a production rate of two per week from February of that year.

ROBIN HR 200 ACROBIN

Dimensions: Span, 27 ft 6½ in (8,40 m); length, 21 ft 11 in (6,68 m); height, 7 ft 1¾ in (2,18 m); wing area, 135·6 sq ft (12,6 m²).

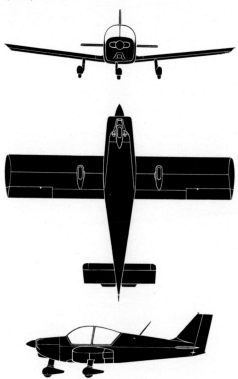

SAAB 35X DRAKEN

Country of Origin: Sweden.

Type: Single-seat multi-purpose fighter.

Power Plant: One 12,710 lb (5 765 kg) dry and 17,260 lb (7 830 kg) reheat Volvo Flygmotor RM 6C (Rolls-Royce RB 146 Mk. 60 Avon) turbojet.

Performance: Max. speed without external stores, 1,320 mph (2 125 km/h) or Mach 2·0 at 36,090 ft (11 000 m), with two 1,000-lb (453,5-kg) bombs and two 280 Imp gal (1 270 l) drop tanks, 925 mph (1 490 km/h) or Mach 1·4; tactical radius for hi-lo-hi mission profile without external fuel, 395 mls (635 km), with two 1,000-lb (453,5-kg) bombs and two 280 Imp gal (1 270 l) drop tanks, 620 mls (1 000 km); ferry range with four 280 Imp gal (1 270 l) drop tanks, 2,015 mls (3 245 km); initial climb, 34,450 ft/min (175 m/sec).

Weights: Loaded (clean aircraft), 25,130 lb (11 400 kg); max. take-off, 35,275 lb (16 000 kg).

Armament: Two 30-mm Aden M/55 cannon and up to 9,000 lb (4 082 kg) of ordnance distributed between nine external stations (six under wings and three under fuselage).

Status: Development airframe flown summer 1967, and first production Saab 35X (for Denmark) flown January 29, 1970.

Notes: The Saab 35X is an export version of the basic Draken (see Saab 35F, 1970 edition) ordered by Denmark and Finland. Denmark took delivery of the last of 40 single-seat Saab 35XDs and six two-seat Saab 35XTs late in 1971, and 12 single-seat Saab XSs have been ordered by Finland with deliveries commencing in 1974. One of six earlier model Saab 35Bs leased to Finland is illustrated above.

SAAB 35X DRAKEN

Dimensions: Span, 30 ft 10¾ in (9,40 m); length, 46 ft 10¼ in (14,28 m); height, 12 ft 8⅓ in (3,89 m); wing area, 529·6 sq ft (49,2 m²).

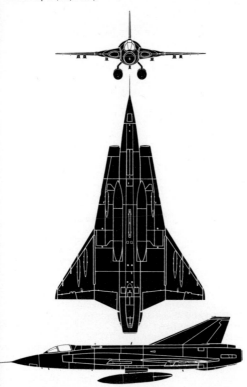

SAAB 37 VIGGEN

Country of Origin: Sweden.

Type: Single-seat multi-purpose fighter and two-seat operational trainer.

Power Plant: One 14,700 lb (6 667 kg) dry and 26,450 lb (12 000 kg) reheat Volvo Flygmotor RM 8 (Pratt & Whitney JT8D-22) turbofan.

Performance: (Estimated) Max. speed without external stores, 1,320 mph (2 125 km/h) or Mach 2·0 at 36,090 ft (11 000 m), 875 mph (1 410 km/h) or Mach 1·15 at 305 ft (100 m); tactical radius with typical external ordnance load for hi-lo-hi mission profile, 620 mls (1 000 km), for lo-lo-lo mission profile, 310 mls (500 km); time to 36,090 ft (11 000 m), 2 min.

Weights: Normal max. take-off, 35,275 lb (16 000 kg).

Armament: All ordnance carried on seven external stores stations (four beneath wings and three under fuselage), primary armament being RB 04E or RB 05A ASMs for the attack role, or RB 24 (Didewinder) or RB 28 (Falcon) AAMs for the intercept role.

Status: First of six single-seat prototypes flown February 8, 1967, and two-seat prototype of training version flown July 2, 1970. Orders placed by beginning of 1972 for 150 single-seat (AJ 37) and 25 two-seat (SK 37) Viggens. First production Viggen flown February 23, 1971, and deliveries to Swedish Air Force began June 21, 1971.

Notes: AJ 37 is primarily an attack aircraft with secondary intercept capability. Future versions include S 37 recce aircraft and JA 37 interceptor with an uprated RM 8B turbofan, new avionics, a built-in 30-mm Oerlikon KCA cannon and long-range missiles. The JA 37 is scheduled to commence its flight test programme in February 1975.

198

SAAB 37 VIGGEN

Dimensions: Span, 34 ft 9¼ in (10,60 m); length, 50 ft 8¼ in (15,45 m), including probe, 53 ft 5¾ in (16,30 m); height, 18 ft 4½ in (5,60 m).

SAAB 105G

Country of Origin: Sweden.
Type: Two-seat light tactical aircraft and basic trainer.
Power Plant: Two 2,850 lb (1 293 kg) General Electric J85-GE-17B turbojets.
Performance: Max. speed, 603 mph (970 km/h) at sea level, 543 mph (875 km/h) at 32,810 ft (10 000 m); range cruise, 435 mph (700 km/h) at 39,370 ft (12 000 m); range (internal fuel with 20 min reserves), 1,230 mls (1 980 km), (with two 88 Imp gal/400 l external tanks and 20 min reserves), 1,570 mls (2 530 km); tactical radius (with six 500-lb/227-kg bombs) for hi-lo-hi mission profile, 432 mls (695 km), for lo-lo-lo mission profile, 186 mls (300 km).
Weights: Empty equipped, 6,801 lb (3 085 kg); max. take-off, 14,330 lb (6 500 kg).
Armament: Four 992-lb (450-kg) and two 606-lb (275-kg) wing hardpoints, typical ordnance loads including six 500-lb (227-kg), four 750-lb (340-kg), or four 992-lb (450-kg) bombs, twelve 13,5-cm rockets, or eight 13,5-cm rockets and two 30-mm cannon pods.
Status: Flown for the first time on May 26, 1972, the Saab 105G is the reworked Saab 105XT prototype (see 1972 edition) originally flown on April 29, 1967.
Notes: The Saab 105G multi-role aircraft which was being offered for export at the beginning of 1973 is a derivative of the experimental Saab 105XT offering increased armament capability, more advanced avionics and improved combat manœuvrability. The side-by-side ejection seats may be replaced by four fixed seats for the liaison role.

SAAB 105G

Dimensions: Span, 31 ft 2 in (9,50 m); length, 35 ft 5⅛ in (10,80 m); height, 8 ft 10¼ in (2,70 m); wing area, 175·45 sq ft (16,30 m²).

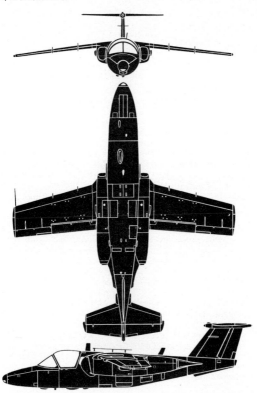

SAAB-MFI 17

Country of Origin: Sweden.

Type: Two-seat light utility, training and counter-insurgency aircraft.

Power Plant: One 200 hp Avco Lycoming IO-360-A1B6 four-cylinder horizontally-opposed engine.

Performance: Max. speed, 163 mph (262 km/h) at sea level; cruise at 75% power, 148 mph (238 km/h) at sea level; max. endurance at sea level (with 10% reserves), 4·75 hrs; max. climb rate, 1,555 ft/min (7,9 m/sec); service ceiling, 22,800 ft (6 950 m).

Weights: Empty equipped, 1,323 lb (600 kg); max. take-off, 2,094 lb.

Armament: Six underwing hardpoints of which two inboard stressed for 220 lb (100 kg) and remainder for 110 lb (50 kg). Typical loads include four Abel pods each with seven 2·75-in (70-mm) HV rockets, six Bantam anti-tank missiles, 18 75-mm Bofors rockets or various types of gun pod.

Status: Prototype MFI 17 flown early summer 1972 with first production deliveries scheduled for spring 1973.

Notes: The Saab-MFI 17 is a more powerful structurally strengthened development of the MFI 15 (see 1971 edition) intended as a relatively inexpensive frontline support aircraft also suited for use for primary, instrument, aerobatic, navigation and weapons training. Space aft of the side-by-side seats may be occupied by a third seat facing to port, access and egress being provided by an upward-hinging door. The Saab-MFI 17 is being offered with both a tricycle undercarriage and a tailwheel arrangement.

SAAB-MFI 17

Dimensions: Span, 28 ft 6½ in (8,70 m); length, 22 ft 11½ in (7,00 m); height, 8 ft 6¼ in (2,60 m); wing area, 127 sq ft (11,8 m²).

SCOTTISH AVIATION BULLDOG 100

Country of Origin: United Kingdom.
Type: Side-by-side two-seat primary trainer.
Power Plant: One 200 hp Lycoming IO-360-A1B6 four-cylinder horizontally-opposed engine.
Performance: Max. speed, 150 mph (240 km/h) at sea level; max. cruise, 138 mph (222 km/h) at 4,000 ft (1 220 m); econ. cruise, 121 mph (194 km/h) at 4,000 ft (1 220 m); max. range, 628 mls (1 010 km) at 4,000 ft (1 220 m); initial climb, 1,100 ft/min (5,58 m/sec); service ceiling, 17,000 ft (5 180 m).
Weights: Empty, 1,420 lb (644 kg); max. take-off, 2,350 lb (1 065 kg).
Status: Beagle-built first prototype flown May 19, 1969. Scottish Aviation-built definitive prototype flying on February 14, 1971, with first production aircraft following July 1971.
Notes: Originally designed by the now-liquidated Beagle Aircraft, the Bulldog was taken over by Scottish Aviation, which has developed the aircraft for production. Production orders have been fulfilled for the Kenya (five Bulldog 103s), Royal Malaysian (15 Bulldog 102s) and Swedish (58 Bulldog 101s) air forces, and the Swedish Army (20), and an order for 132 for the RAF was placed in 1972. The RAF model, the Bulldog 120, will be structurally strengthened to increase the fully aerobatic weight, and a wider range of instruments and avionics will be provided. First deliveries of the Bulldog 120 were scheduled for March–April 1973.

SCOTTISH AVIATION BULLDOG

Dimensions: Span, 33 ft 0 in (10,06 m); length, 23 ft 2½ in (7,07 m); height, 7 ft 5¾ in (2,28 m); wing area, 129·4 sq ft (12,02 m²).

SCOTTISH AVIATION JETSTREAM 200

Country of Origin: United Kingdom.

Type: Light business executive and utility transport.

Power Plant: Two 940 eshp Turboméca Astazou XVI turbo-props.

Performance: Max. cruise, 285 mph (459 km/h) at 12,000 ft (3 660 m); range with max. fuel and 5% reserves plus 45 min hold, 1,382 mls (2 224 km); initial climb, 2,500 ft/min (12,7 m/sec).

Weights: Empty equipped (executive), 9,286 lb (4 212 kg); max. take-off, 12,500 lb (5 670 kg).

Accommodation: Normal flight crew of two and 12 passengers in executive layout with alternative 12–18 passenger commuter arrangements.

Status: Development initiated by Handley Page as the Jetstream 2, and flight testing resumed by Jetstream Aircraft Limited as the Jetstream Series 200 in December 1970. Production subsequently taken over by Scottish Aviation. Delivery of 26 pilot-training aircraft to the RAF to commence mid-1973.

Notes: The initial Handley Page-built version was the Jetstream 1 with Astazou XIV engines, 36 production examples of which were completed. Development of the Astazou XVI-powered Jetstream 2 was initiated by Handley Page with the re-engined first pre-production aircraft. Jetstream Aircraft was formed to take over the development, production and marketing of the HP 137 Jetstream following the demise of the Handley Page company. All development and production is now being undertaken by Scottish Aviation.

SCOTTISH AVIATION JETSTREAM 200

Dimensions: Span, 52 ft 0 in (15,85 m); length, 47 ft 1½ in (14,37 m); height, 17 ft 5½ in (5,32 m); wing area, 270 sq ft (25,08 m²).

SEPECAT JAGUAR G.R. MK. 1

Countries of Origin: France and United Kingdom.
Type: Single-seat tactical strike fighter.
Power Plant: Two 4,620 lb (2 100 kg) dry and 7,140 lb (3 240 kg) reheat Rolls-Royce Turboméca RT.172 Adour 102 turbofans.
Performance: (At typical weight) Max. speed, 820 mph (1 320 km/h) or Mach 1·1 at 1,000 ft (305 m), 1,057 mph (1 700 km/h) or Mach 1·6 at 32,810 ft (10 000 m); cruise with max. ordnance, 430 mph (690 km/h) or Mach 0·65 at 39,370 ft (12 000 m); range with external fuel for lo-lo-lo mission profile, 450 mls (724 km), for hi-lo-hi mission profile, 710 mls (1 142 km); ferry range, 2,270 mls (3 650 km).
Weights: Normal take-off, 23,000 lb (10 430 kg); max. take-off, 32,600 lb (14 790 kg).
Armament: Two 30-mm Aden cannon and up to 10,000 lb (4 536 kg) ordnance on five external hardpoints.
Status: First of eight prototypes flown September 8, 1968. First production Jaguar E for France flown November 2, 1971, with first Jaguar A following April 20, 1972. First production Jaguar S for UK flown October 11, 1972.
Notes: Both France and UK have a requirement for approximately 200 Jaguars, French versions being the single-seat A (*Appui Tactique*) and two-seat E (*École de Combat*), and British versions being the single-seat S (G.R. Mk. 1) and the two-seat B (T Mk. 2), current plans calling for the delivery of 165 single-seaters and 35 two-seaters to the RAF. The G.R. Mk. 1 differs from the Jaguar A in having a nose-mounted laser rangefinder and tail-mounted avionics pack.

SEPECAT JAGUAR G.R. MK. 1

Dimensions: Span, 28 ft 6 in (8,69 m); length, 50 ft 11 in (15,52 m); height, 16 ft 0½ in (4,89 m); wing area, 260·3 sq ft (24,18 m²).

SHIN MEIWA SS-2 (PS-1)

Country of Origin: Japan.

Type: Long-range maritime patrol flying boat.

Power Plant: Four 3,060 ehp Ishikawajima-built General Electric T64-IHI-10 turboprops.

Performance: Max. speed, 340 mph (547 km/h) at 5,000 ft (1 525 m); normal cruise, 265 mph (426 km/h) at 5,000 ft (1 525 m); normal range, 1,347 mls (2 168 km); ferry range, 2,948 mls (4 744 km); max. endurance, 15 hrs; initial climb, 2,264 ft/min (6,89 m/sec); service ceiling, 29,530 ft (9 000 m).

Weights: Empty equipped, 58,000 lb (26 300 kg); normal take-off, 79,366 lb (36 000 kg); max. take-off, 99,208 lb (45 000 kg).

Armament: Four 330-lb (150-kg) anti-submarine bombs on upper deck and additional weapons enclosed in two under-wing pods between engine nacelles (each containing two homing torpedoes) and a launcher beneath each wingtip (for three 5-in/12,7-cm rockets).

Accommodation: Two pilots and engineer on flight deck and seven additional crew members in tactical compartment on upper deck.

Status: First of two prototypes flown October 5, 1967, these being followed in 1972 by two pre-production examples. Initial batch of five production SS-2s for delivery during 1973 and a further nine during the current five-year (1972–76) defence programme.

Notes: Three examples of an amphibious search and rescue version of the SS-2, the SS-2A, are currently on order for the Maritime Self-Defence Force.

SHIN MEIWA SS-2 (PS-1)

Dimensions: Span, 108 ft 8¾ in (33,14 m); length, 109 ft 11 in (33,50 m); height, 31 ft 10½ in (9,71 m); wing area, 1,462 sq ft (135,8 m²).

SHORT SKYVAN SERIES 3M

Country of Origin: United Kingdom.
Type: Light military utility transport.
Power Plant: Two 715 shp Garrett AiResearch TPE 331-201 turboprops.
Performance: Max. cruise, 201 mph (323 km/h) at 10,000 ft (3 050 m); econ. cruise, 173 mph (278 km/h) at 10,000 ft (3 050 m); range with max. fuel and 45 min reserves, 660 mls (1 062 km), with 5,000-lb (2 268-kg) payload and same reserves, 166 mls (267 km); initial climb, 1,520 ft/min (7,6 m/sec); service ceiling, 21,000 ft (6 400 m).
Weights: Basic operational, 7,400 lb (3 356 kg); max. take-off, 14,500 lb (6 577 kg).
Accommodation: Flight crew of one or two, and up to 22 fully-equipped troops, 16 paratroops and a despatcher, or 12 casualty stretchers and two medical attendants.
Status: Series 3M prototype flown early in 1970, and six delivered during course of year to Sultan of Oman's Air Force, this order being supplemented by orders for a further four. Five ordered for Argentine Navy, two for Nepalese Army, six for the Singapore Air Defence and one being ordered by the Ecuador Army. Interspersed on assembly line with civil Series 3, and combined production running at two per month at beginning of 1973 with some 76 ordered of both versions.
Notes: The Series 3M embodies features incorporated in two Skyvans supplied to the Austrian Air Force.

SHORT SKYVAN SERIES 3M

Dimensions: Span, 64 ft 11 in (19,79 m); length, 40 ft 1 in (12,21 m), with radome, 41 ft 4 in (12,60 m); height, 15 ft 1 in (4,60 m); wing area, 373 sq ft (34,65 m²).

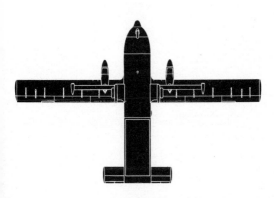

SIAI-MARCHETTI S.208

Country of Origin: Italy.

Type: Light cabin monoplane.

Power Plant: One 260 hp Avco Lycoming O-540-E4A5 six-cylinder horizontally-opposed engine.

Performance: Max. speed, 177 mph (285 km/h) at sea level; cruise at 75% power, 161 mph (260 km/h) at 6,560 ft (2 000 m), at 65% power, 151 mph (243 km/h) at 1,970 ft (600 m); range at 60% power, 1,118 mls (1 800 km); service ceiling, 17,716 ft (5 400 m).

Weights: Empty equipped, 1,823 lb (827 kg); max. take-off, 3,310 lb (1 502 kg).

Accommodation: Pilot and four passengers in individual seats (two side-by-side pairs and single seat at rear and to port.

Status: Prototype flown on May 22, 1967, with production deliveries commencing during 1968. Forty-four examples of a military version, the S.208M, supplied to the Italian Air Force.

Notes: The S.208 possesses some 60 per cent structural component commonality with the lower-powered S.205, a four-seater with a 200 hp Avco Lycoming IO-360-A1A engine and both fixed (S.205-20/F) and retractable (S.205-20/R) undercarriage, production of which is now complete. The military S.208M differs from the standard civil production model primarily in having a jettisonable cabin door and is employed for both liaison and training tasks.

SIAI-MARCHETTI S.208

Dimensions: Span, 36 ft 10 in (11,24 m); length, 26 ft 7 in (8,09 m); height, 9 ft 6 in (2,89 m); wing area, 173 sq ft (16,09 m²).

SIAI-MARCHETTI S.210

Country of Origin: Italy.
Type: Light cabin monoplane.
Power Plant: Two 200 hp Lycoming TIO-360-A1B four-cylinder horizontally-opposed engines.
Performance: Max. speed, 233 mph (375 km/h) at 18,700 ft (5 700 m); cruise at 75% power, 215 mph (346 km/h) at 18,700 ft (5 700 m); max. range, 1,180 mls (1 190 km); initial climb, 1,560 ft/min (7,92 m/sec).
Weights: Empty equipped, 2,359 lb (1 070 kg); max. take-off, 4,078 lb (1 850 kg).
Accommodation: Pilot and five passengers in three pairs of side-by-side seats.
Status: First of two prototypes flown February 18, 1970, and work initiated on pre-production series of 10 airframes.
Notes: A twin-engined derivative of the S.205—S.208 range of single-engined light cabin monoplanes and possessing extensive structural component commonality with its predecessors, the S.210 has been under development for several years, prototype trials being delayed by the priority attached to establishing the company's single-engined line. The second prototype differs from that illustrated above in having staggered entry doors (rear port, front starboard), an enlarged baggage compartment door, and enlarged rear windows. One prototype re-engined with Continental Tiara engines early 1973, the roof-line being lowered simultaneously.

SIAI-MARCHETTI S.210

Dimensions: Span, 38 ft 2 in (11,63 m); length, 28 ft 11$\frac{7}{8}$ in (8,83 m); height, 10 ft 1$\frac{3}{4}$ in (3,09 m); wing area, 185·5 sq ft (17,23 m²).

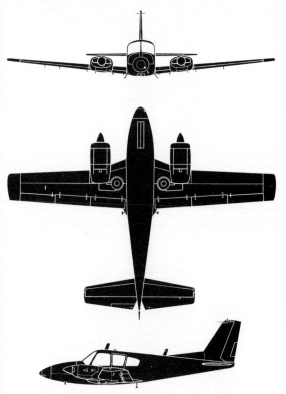

SIAI-MARCHETTI SF.260W WARRIOR

Country of Origin: Italy.

Type: Side-by-side two-seat light tactical and training aircraft.

Power Plant: One 260 hp Avco Lycoming O-540-E4A5 six-cylinder horizontally-opposed engine.

Performance: (Without external stores) Max. speed, 230 mph (370 km/h) at sea level; max. cruise, 214 mph (345 km/h) at 10,000 ft (3 050 m); econ. cruise, 203 mph (327 km/h) at 10,000 ft (3 050 m); max. range, 1,275 mls (2 050 km); initial climb, 1,770 ft/min (10 m/sec); service ceiling, 21,370 ft (6 500 m).

Weights: Empty equipped, 1,764 lb (800 kg); max. take-off, 2,879–2998 lb (1 306–1 360 kg).

Armament: Stores pylons for maximum of 661 lb (300 kg) of ordnance. Typical ordnance loads comprise two Matra gun pods each containing two 7,62-mm MAC AAF1 machine guns, two Alkan 20AP cartridge throwers, two Simpres AL18-50 pods each containing 18 2-in (5,0-cm) rockets or AL9-70 pods each containing nine 2·75-in (6,98-cm) rockets, or two 110-lb (50-kg) or 264·5-lb (120-kg) bombs.

Status: The prototype SF.260W was flown for the first time in May 1972. Production rate of 6–8 SF.260s per month at beginning of 1973.

Notes: The Warrior is an armed version of the SF.260MX trainer, the generic designation of the export military version of the SF.260 cabin monoplane of which deliveries commenced in 1970. The SF.260MX has been supplied to Belgium (36), Zaïre (12), Zambia (10), Singapore (18), Philippines (6) and Thailand (12 plus an option on a further 12).

SIAI-MARCHETTI SF.260W WARRIOR

Dimensions: Span, 26 ft 11¾ in (8,25 m); length, 23 ft 0 in (7,02 m); height, 8 ft 6 in (2,60 m); wing area, 108·5 sq ft (10,1 m²).

SIAI-MARCHETTI SM.1019A

Country of Origin: Italy.

Type: Battlefield surveillance and forward air control aircraft.

Power Plant: One 317 shp Allison 250-B15G turboprop.

Performance: Max. speed, 188 mph (302 km/h) at 6,000 ft (1 830 m); max. cruise, 173 mph (278 km/h) at 6,000 ft (1 830 m); econ. cruise, 135 mph (217 km/h) at 10,000 ft (3 050 m); range with max. fuel and 10 min reserves, 765 mls (1 230 km), with 500-lb (227-kg) external stores on wing stations and same reserves, 320 mls (515 km); initial climb, 1,625 ft (8,25 m/sec).

Weights: Empty equipped, 1,480 lb (672 kg); max. take-off, 2,513 lb (1 140 kg).

Armament: Two stores stations under wings capable of carrying minigun pods, rockets, etc., up to a maximum external load of 500 lb (227 kg).

Status: First of two prototypes flown May 24, 1969 and second on July 14, 1970. A production line for 100 aircraft was being laid down late 1972.

Notes: The SM.1019 is based upon the Cessna O-1 Bird Dog but possesses an extensively modified airframe to meet latest operational requirements, redesigned tail surfaces, and a turboprop in place of the O-1's piston engine. The second prototype, the SM.1019A, has a second door for the observer and duplicated instrument panel. The SM.1019 competed with the AM.3C (see pages 6–7) for a production order for the Italian Army, and was selected as the winning contender. The SM.1019A will be delivered to the Italian Army during 1973–74.

SIAI-MARCHETTI SM.1019A

Dimensions: Span, 36 ft 0 in (10,97 m); length, 27 ft 8 in (8,43 m); height, 7 ft 9¾ in (2,38 m); wing area, 173·94 sq ft (16,16 m²).

SUKHOI SU-7MF (FITTER)

Country of Origin: USSR.

Type: Single-seat ground attack fighter.

Power Plant: One (approx.) 22,050 lb (10 000 kg) reheat Lyulka AL-7F-1 turbojet.

Performance: (Estimated) Max. speed without external stores, 720 mph (1 160 km/h) or Mach 0·95 at 1,000 ft (305 m), 1,056 mph (1 700 km/h) at 39,370 ft (12 000 m), in high-drag configuration (e.g. two rocket pods and two 132 Imp gal/600 l drop tanks), 790 mph (1 270 km/h) or Mach 1·2 at 39,370 ft (12 000 m); combat radius for hi-lo-hi mission profile, 285 mls (460 km); initial climb without external stores, 29,500 ft/min (150 m/sec).

Weights: (Estimated) Normal take-off, 26,455 lb (12 000 kg); max. take-off, 30,865 lb (14 000 kg).

Armament: Two 30-mm NR-30 cannon and such loads as two 550-lb (250-kg) bombs and two UV-16-57 pods each containing 16 55-mm rockets distributed between four external stores stations (two under wings and two under fuselage).

Status: Prototypes allegedly flown 1955 with production deliveries of initial service version to the Soviet Air Forces commencing 1958.

Notes: The Su-7 has been widely exported, the latest single-seat production model reportedly being the Su-7MF with up-rated engine and improved short-field characteristics. Among countries employing this type are India, Egypt, Iraq and Syria. A tandem two-seat conversion trainer variant, the Su-7U, dubbed Moujik by NATO (see 1970 edition) is also in service.

SUKHOI SU-7MF (FITTER)

Dimensions: (Estimated) Span, 31 ft 2 in (9,50 m); length, 55 ft 9 in (17,00 m); height, 15 ft 5 in (4,70 m).

SUKHOI SU-9MF (FISHPOT)

Country of Origin: USSR.

Type: Single-seat all-weather interceptor.

Power Plant: One (approx.) 22,050 lb (10 000 kg) reheat Lyulka AL-7F turbojet.

Performance: (Estimated) Max. speed without external stores, 720 mph (1 160 km/h) or Mach 0·95 at 1,000 ft (305 m), 1,190 mph (1 915 km/h) or Mach 1·8 at 40,000 ft (12 190 m), (high-drag configuration—two Anab AAMs and two 132 Imp gal/600 l drop tanks), 790 mph (1 270 km/h) at Mach 1·2 at 40,000 ft (12 190 m); initial climb, 27,000 ft/min (137 m/sec); service ceiling, 55,000 ft (16 765 m).

Weights: (Estimated) Normal take-off, 25,500 lb (11 567 kg); max., 30,000 lb (13 608 kg).

Armament: Two advanced Anab AAMs.

Status: Prototypes of the Su-9 were initially flown in the mid 'fifties, initial production version entering service with the Soviet Air Forces during the early 'sixties. The Su-9 has since been manufactured in progressively improved versions.

Notes: The Su-9 originally possessed some component commonality with the Su-7 (see pages 222–223), the fuselages, power plants and tail assemblies of the two aircraft being similar. More powerful versions of the AL-7F, more advanced avionics and more sophisticated missile armament have been progressively introduced, the final production model apparently being the Su-9MF, and a tandem two-seat conversion training variant, the Su-9U, dubbed *Maiden* by NATO, is illustrated on the opposite page.

SUKHOI SU-9U (MAIDEN)

Dimensions: (Estimated) Span, 31 ft 0 in (9,45 m); length, 55 ft 0 in (16,76 m); height, 16 ft 0 in (4,88 m); wing area, 425 sq ft (39,48 m²).

SUKHOI SU-11 (FLAGON-A)

Country of Origin: USSR.

Type: Single-seat all-weather interceptor fighter.

Power Plant: Two (approx.) 25,000 lb (11 340 kg) reheat Lyulka AL- 9 turbojets.

Performance: (Estimated) Max. speed without external stores, 1,650 mph (2 655 km/h) or Mach 2·5 at 39,370 ft (12 000 m), 910 mph (1 465 km/h) or Mach 1·2 at 1,000 ft (305 m), with AAMs on wing stations and twin drop tanks on fuselage stations, 1,120 mph (1 800 km/h) or Mach 1·7 at 39,370 ft (12 000 m); range at subsonic cruise with max. external fuel, 1,500 mls (2 415 km).

Weights: (Estimated) Normal take-off, 35,000–40,000 lb (15 875–18 145 kg).

Armament: Basic armament for intercept mission reportedly comprises two AAMs of Anab type on wing stations, but various ordnance loads may be carried for the attack role, these being distributed between two fuselage and two wing stations.

Status: The Su-11 is believed to have flown in prototype form during 1964–65 with production deliveries commencing 1969, and some 400 were alleged by US official sources to be in service with the Soviet Air Forces by mid-1971 when production was believed to be some 15 aircraft monthly.

Notes: Apparently optimised for the intercept role as a successor to the Su-9 (see pages 224–225), the Su-11 is in large-scale service with the Soviet Air Forces. A STOL version with three direct lift engines mounted vertically in the centre fuselage, the Flagon-B, is illustrated above but is of uncertain status, although unofficial reports during 1972 suggested that it is in operational service on a limited scale.

SUKHOI SU-11 (FLAGON-A)

Dimensions: (Estimated) Span, 31 ft 3 in (9,50 m); length, 70 ft 6 in (21,50 m); height, 16 ft 6 in (5,00 m).

TUPOLEV TU-22 (BLINDER)

Country of Origin: USSR.

Type: Long-range medium bomber and strike-reconnaissance aircraft.

Power Plant: Two (approx.) 27,000 lb (12 250 kg) reheat turbojets.

Performance: (Estimated) Max. speed without external stores, 990 mph (1 590 km/h) or Mach 1·5 at 39,370 ft (12 000 m), 720 mph (1 160 km/h) or Mach 0·95 at 1,000 ft (305 m); normal cruise, 595 mph (960 km/h) or Mach 0·9 at 39,370 ft (12 000 m); tactical radius on standard fuel for high-altitude mission, 700 mls (1 125 km); service ceiling, 60,000 ft (18 290 m).

Weights: (Estimated) Max. take-off, 185,000 lb (84 000 kg).

Armament: Free-falling weapons housed internally or (Blinder-B) semi-recessed Kitchen ASM. Remotely-controlled 23-mm cannon in tail barbette.

Status: Believed to have attained operational status with the Soviet Air Forces in 1965.

Notes: The Tu-22 is the successor to the subsonic Tu-16 in Soviet medium-bomber formations and with shore-based maritime strike elements of the Soviet Naval Air Arm. The basic version is dubbed Blinder-A by NATO, the missile-carrying Blinder-B being illustrated on the opposite page. A training version, the Blinder-C (illustrated above), features a raised second cockpit for the instructor. Recent production models of the Tu-22 display a number of modifications, including an extended flight refuelling probe and enlarged engine air intakes, nacelles and exhaust orifices.

TUPOLEV TU-22 (BLINDER)

Dimensions: (Estimated) Span, 91 ft 0 in (27,74 m); length, 133 ft 0 in (40,50 m); height, 17 ft 0 in (5,18 m); wing area, 2,030 sq ft (188,59 m²).

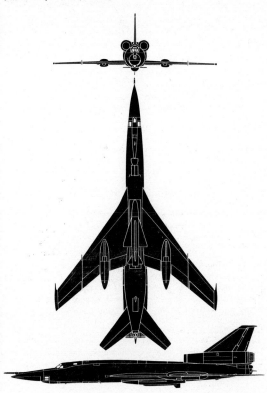

TUPOLEV (MOSS)

Country of Origin: USSR.

Type: Airborne warning and control system aircraft.

Power Plant: Four 14,795 ehp Kuznetsov NK-12MV turbo-props.

Performance: (Estimated) Max. continuous cruise, 460 mph (740 km/h) at 25,000 ft (7 620 m); max. unrefuelled range, 4,000+ mls (6 440+ km); service ceiling, 39,000 ft (11 890 m).

Weights: (Estimated) Normal max. take-off, 360,000 lb (163 290 kg).

Accommodation: Operational crew is likely to comprise 15–20 personnel.

Status: The AWACS aircraft assigned the reporting name *Moss* by the Air Standards Co-ordinating Committee became known to Western intelligence agencies in the mid 'sixties, and first appeared in service with the Soviet Air Forces in 1970.

Notes: Essentially an adaptation of the Tu-114 commercial transport, and apparently retaining the wings, tail surfaces, power plant and undercarriage of the earlier aircraft, the Tupolev AWACS type is primarily intended to locate low-flying intruders and to vector interceptors towards them. The dominating feature of the aircraft is its pylon-mounted saucer-shaped early-warning scanner housing of approximately 37·5 ft (12,00 m) diameter. An externally-faired fuel line runs aft from the refuelling probe along the starboard side of the fuselage, and there are various sensor-housing blisters on the fuselage and at the tailplane tips.

TUPOLEV (MOSS)

Dimensions: Span, 168 ft 0 in (51,20 m); approx. length, 188 ft 0 in (57,30 m); height, 51 ft 0 in (15,50 m); wing area, 3,349 sq ft (311,1 m²).

TUPOLEV TU-134A (CRUSTY)

Country of Origin: USSR.

Type: Short- to medium-range commercial transport.

Power Plant: Two 14,990 lb (6 800 kg) Soloviev D-30-2 Turbofans.

Performance: Max. cruise, 528 mph (850 km/h) at 32,810 ft (10 000 m); long-range cruise, 466 mph (750 km/h) at 32,810 ft (10 000 m); max. range at long-range cruise with 1 hr reserves and 18,108-lb (8 215-kg) payload, 1,243 mls (2 000 km), with 8,818-lb (4 000-kg) payload, 2,175 mls (3 500 km).

Weights: Operational empty, 63,934 lb (29 000 kg); max. take-off, 103,617 lb (47 000 kg).

Accommodation: Basic flight crew of three and maximum of 80 passengers in four-abreast all-tourist class configuration.

Status: Prototype Tu-134A flown in 1968 and first production deliveries (to *Aeroflot*) mid-1970. Series production continuing at Kharkov at the beginning of 1973.

Notes: The Tu-134A differs from the original Tu-134, which entered *Aeroflot* service in 1966, in having an additional 6 ft 10⅔ in (2,10 m) section inserted in the fuselage immediately forward of the wing to permit two additional rows of passenger seats, and introduces engine thrust reversers. Maximum take-off weight has been increased by 5,512 lb (2 500 kg), maximum payload being raised by 1,025 lb (465 kg), an APU is provided, and radio and navigational equipment have been revised. Route proving trials with the Tu-134A were completed by *Aeroflot* late in 1970, and this airliner was introduced on international routes early in 1971. The shorter-fuselage Tu-134 (illustrated above) serves with CSA, Interflug, LOT, Malev, Bulair, Balkan-Bulgarian and Aviogenex.

TUPOLEV TU-134A (CRUSTY)

Dimensions: Span, 95 ft 2 in (29,00 m); length, 111 ft 0½ in (36,40 m); height, 29 ft 7 in (9,02 m); wing area, 1,370·3 sq ft (127,3 m²).

TUPOLEV TU-144 (CHARGER)

Country of Origin: USSR.

Type: Long-range supersonic commercial transport.

Power Plant: Four 28,660 lb (13 000 kg) dry and 38,580 lb (17 500 kg) Kuznetsov NK-144 turbofans.

Performance: (Estimated) Max. cruise, 1,550 mph (2 500 km/h) or Mach 2·35 between 49,200 and 65,600 ft (15 000 and 20 000 m); range with max. payload, 4,040 mls (6 500 km).

Weights: Max. take-off, 396,830 lb (180 000 kg).

Accommodation: Basic flight crew of three, and mixed-class arrangement for 82 tourist-class and 18 first-class passengers, or all-tourist arrangements for up to 140 passengers.

Status: First prototype commenced flight test programme on December 31, 1968. First of two production prototypes joined the development programme during September 1971, the second of these (illustrated above) being representative of the production configuration.

Notes: The Tu-144 possesses the distinction of having been the world's first commercial transport to exceed both Mach 1·0 (on June 5, 1969) and Mach 2·0 (on May 26, 1970), reaching 1,336 mph (2 150 km/h), or Mach 2·02, at 53,500 ft (16 300 m) during the latter flight. The pre-production prototype (illustrated above) differs in a number of respects from the first prototype (opposite page), changes including revised engine air-intake geometry, repositioned main undercarriage members, modified cockpit vizor, alterations to the distribution of the spanwise wing camber and the introduction of retractable foreplanes.

TUPOLEV TU-144 (CHARGER)

Dimensions: (First prototype) Span, 90 ft 8½ in (27,65 m); length (excluding probe), 194 ft 10½ in (59,40 m).

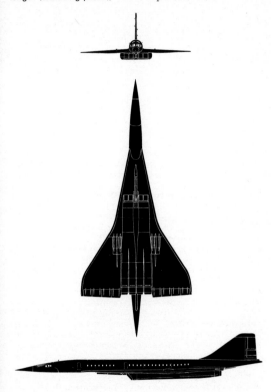

TUPOLEV TU-154 (CARELESS)

Country of Origin: USSR.

Type: Medium- to long-range commercial transport.

Power Plant: Three 20,950 lb (9 500 kg) Kuznetsov NK-8-2 turbofans.

Performance: Max. cruise, 605 mph (975 km/h) at 31,170 ft (9 500 m); long-range cruise, 528 mph (850 km/h) at 37,730 ft (11 500 m); range with standard fuel and reserves of 1 hr plus 6% and max. payload, 2,150 mls (3 460 km) at 560 mph (900 km/h), 2,360 mls (3 800 km) at 528 mph (850 km/h).

Weights: Operational empty, 95,900 lb (43 500 kg); normal take-off, 185,188 lb (84 000 kg); max. take-off, 198,416 lb (90 000 kg).

Accommodation: Basic flight crew of three–four, and alternative arrangements for 158 or 150 economy-class passengers, 150, 146 or 136 tourist-class passengers, or 24 first-class and 104 tourist-class passengers.

Status: First prototype flown October 4, 1968, with first delivery of a production aircraft (to *Aeroflot*) following August 1970, route proving commencing August 1971.

Notes: The Tu-154 entered service on *Aeroflot* routes early 1972, and is intended as a successor to the Tu-104, Il-18 and An-10 on medium- to long-range routes. It can operate from airfields with category B surfaces, including packed earth and gravel. Operators include Aviogenex of Yugoslavia, CSA of Czechoslovakia, Balkan Bulgarian, and Interflug of East Germany. A growth version, referred to as the Tu-154M, is currently under development, flight testing having been scheduled for late 1972. This model incorporates additional fuselage sections which will enable 220–240 passengers to be carried, and has uprated NK-8 turbofans.

TUPOLEV TU-154 (CARELESS)

Dimensions: Span, 123 ft 2½ in (37,55 m); length, 157 ft 1¾ in (47,90 m); height, 37 ft 4¾ in (11,40 m); wing area, 2,168·92 sq ft (201,45 m²).

VFW-FOKKER VFW 614

Country of Origin: Federal Germany.
Type: Short-range commercial transport.
Power Plant: Two 7,510 (3 410 kg) Rolls-Royce/SNECMA M45H turbofans.
Performance: (Estimated) Max. speed, 457 mph (735 km/h) at 21,000 ft (6 400 m); max. cruise, 449 mph (722 km/h) at 25,000 ft (7 620 m); long-range cruise, 390 mph (627 km/h) at 25,000 ft (7 620 m); range with max. fuel, 1,145 mls (1 845 km), with max. payload, 390 mls (630 km); initial climb rate, 3,248 ft min (16,5 m/sec).
Weights: Operational empty, 26,896 lb (12 000 kg); max. take-off, 41,006 lb (18 600 kg).
Accommodation: Basic flight crew of two and alternative passenger configurations for 36, 40 or 44 seats in four-abreast rows.
Status: First of three prototypes commenced its flight test programme on June 14, 1971, with second and third following on August 19 and October 10, 1972. First production aircraft scheduled to be delivered during 1974.
Notes: The VFW 614 is being manufactured as a collaborative venture under the leadership of VFW-Fokker, participants including the Dutch Fokker-VFW concern and the Belgian SABCA and Fairey companies. The VFW 614 is intended as an ultra-short-haul DC-3 replacement, and an unconventional feature is its over-wing engine-pod installation. Emphasis has been placed on flexibility of operation in a wide variety of different environments and with a minimum of maintenance.

VFW-FOKKER VFW 614

Dimensions: Span, 70 ft 6½ in (21,50 m); length, 67 ft 7 in (20,60 m); height, 25 ft 8 in (7,84 m); wing area, 688·89 sq ft (64,00 m²).

VOUGHT YA-7H CORSAIR II

Country of Origin: USA.

Type: Tandem two-seat combat crew trainer.

Power Plant: One 15,000 lb (6 804 kg) Allison TF41-A-2 (Rolls-Royce RB.168-62 Spey) turbofan.

Performance: Max. speed (at 33,912 lb/15 383 kg), 618 mph (995 km/h) at sea level; radius of action, 466 mls (750 km); ferry range (no external stores and max. internal fuel), 2,268 mls (3 650 km).

Weights: Empty equipped, 18,821 lb (8 537 kg); normal take-off, 29,410 lb (13 340 kg).

Armament: Provision for one 20-mm M-61A-1 rotary cannon with 1,000 rounds and similar external ordnance loads to those of single-seat A-7E distributed between eight external hardpoints.

Status: Prototype YA-7H flown on August 29, 1972. US Navy preliminary planning for Fiscal 1974 includes an initial order for 12 A-7Hs.

Notes: The YA-7H is a company-funded two-seat derivative of the single-seat A-7E (see 1972 edition) intended primarily for instrument and combat crew training. Retaining the basic A-7E airframe, it features a new, re-faired nose embodying a 16-in (40,64 cm) stretch, an 18-in (45,72-cm) insert just aft of the wing, modified overwing fairings, and a 1·2 deg upward tilt of the aft fuselage. Studies are being undertaken for an advanced attack single-seater based on the YA-7H airframe with the space currently occupied by the aft cockpit being used to store ammunition for a new, larger-calibre cannon. It is likely that this development will couple wing high-lift devices with a Pratt & Whitney F100 turbofan.

VOUGHT YA-7H CORSAIR II

Dimensions: Span, 38 ft 8¾ in (11,80 m); length, 48 ft 5½ in (14,84 m); height, 16 ft 5 in (5,00 m); wing area, 375 sq ft (34,83 m²).

YAKOVLEV YAK-28P (FIREBAR)

Country of Origin: USSR.
Type: Two-seat all-weather interceptor fighter.
Power Plant: Two 10,140 lb (4 600 kg) dry and 13,670 lb (6 200 kg) reheat Tumansky RD-11 turbojets.
Performance: (Estimated) Max. speed without external stores, 760 mph (1 225 km/h) or Mach 1·15 at 39,370 ft (12 000 m), with two Anab AAMs, 695 mph (1 120 km/h) or Mach 1·05; normal cruise, 560 mph (900 km/h) or Mach 0·9; tactical radius for high-altitude patrol mission, 550 mls (885 km); initial climb, 28,000 ft/min (142,2 m/sec); service ceiling, 55,000 ft (16 765 m).
Weights: (Estimated) Normal take-off, 37,480 lb (17 000 kg); max. take-off, 40,785 lb (18 500 kg).
Armament: Standard armament comprises two Anab semi-active radar-homing AAMs carried by stores stations under wing. Some examples have been seen with four wing stores stations for two Anab AAMs and two infra-red homing Atoll AAMs.
Status: Flown in prototype form in 1960 with production deliveries commencing 1963–64.
Notes: The Yak-28P was developed in parallel with the Yak-28 tactical strike-recce aircraft, featuring a dielectric nose cone, tandem seating for the two crew members with windscreen (and twin-wheel forward member of "bicycle" undercarriage) about 2 ft 6 in (76 cm) further forward, and internal weapons bay deleted, this space presumably being occupied by fuel tankage. The Yak-28P is widely used by the Soviet Air Forces, and latest service version (illustrated) features a refined and lengthened nose cone.

YAKOVLEV YAK-28P (FIREBAR)

Dimensions: (Estimated) Span, 44 ft 6 in (13,56 m); length (with probe), 75 ft 0 in (22,86 m), (without probe), 67 ft 0 in (20,42 m); height, 15 ft 0 in (4,57 m).

YAKOVLEV YAK-40 (CODLING)

Country of Origin: USSR.
Type: Short-range commercial feederliner.
Power Plant: Three 3,307 lb (1 500 kg) Ivchenko AI-25 turbofans.
Performance: Max. speed, 373 mph (600 km/h) at sea level, 466 mph (750 km/h) at 17,000 ft (5 180 m); max. cruise, 342 mph (550 km/h) at 19,685 ft (6 000 m); econ. cruise, 310 mph (500 km/h) at 32,810 ft (10 000 m); range with 5,070-lb (2 300-kg) payload at econ. cruise, 620 mls (1 000 km), with 3,140-lb (1 425-kg) payload and max. fuel, 920 mls (1 480 km); initial climb, 2,000 ft/min (10,16 m/sec); service ceiling at max. loaded weight, 38,715 ft (11 800 m).
Weights: Empty equipped, 19,865–21,715 lb (9 010–9 850 kg); normal take-off, 27,250–34,170 lb (12 360–15 500 kg); max. take-off, 36,375 lb (16 500 kg).
Accommodation: Flight crew of two, and alternative arrangements for 27 or 34 passengers in three-abreast rows. High-density arrangement for 40 passengers in four-abreast rows, and business executive configuration for 8–10 passengers.
Status: First of five prototypes flown October 21, 1966, and first production deliveries (to *Aeroflot*) mid-1968. Some 400 delivered by beginning of 1973.
Notes: A thrust reverser introduced as standard on centre engine during 1971 when more powerful version with three 3,858 lb (1 750 kg) AI-25T turbofans and increased fuel capacity announced for 1972 delivery.

YAKOVLEV YAK-40 (CODLING)

Dimensions: Span, 82 ft 0¼ in (25,00 m); length, 66 ft 9½ in (20,36 m); height, 21 ft 4 in (6,50 m); wing area, 753·473 sq ft (70 m²).

AÉROSPATIALE SA 318C ALOUETTE II

Country of Origin: France.

Type: Five-seat light utility helicopter.

Power Plant: One 523 shp Turboméca Astazou IIA turboshaft.

Performance: Max. speed, 127 mph (205 km/h) at sea level; max. cruise, 112 mph (180 km/h); max. inclined climb, 1,396 ft/min (7, 1 m/sec); hovering ceiling (in ground effect), 5,085 ft (1 550 m), (out of ground effect), 2,950 ft (900 m); range with max. fuel, 447 mls (720 km), with max. payload, 62 mls (100 km).

Weights: Empty, 1,961 lb (890 kg); max. take-off, 3,630 lb (1 650 kg).

Dimensions: Rotor diam, 33 ft 5⅝ in (10,20 m); fuselage length, 31 ft 11¾ in (9,75 m).

Notes: The SA 318C has been developed from the SE 313B Alouette II (see 1967 edition) which it has supplanted in production. The earlier model differed primarily in having an Artouste turboshaft, and 923 examples were built. The Astazou offers a 25 per cent improvement in fuel consumption and, together with other design changes, has provided the SA 318C version of the Alouette II with performance improvements and a 375-lb (170-kg) increase in payload. The SA 315B Lama is a version of the Alouette II with an Artouste IIB and mechanical systems of the Alouette III certificated in September 1970.

AÉROSPATIALE SA 319A ALOUETTE III

Country of Origin: France.
Type: Seven-seat light utility helicopter.
Power Plant: One 789 shp Turboméca Astazou XIV turboshaft.
Performance: Max. speed, 137 mph (220 km/h) at sea level; max. cruise, 122 mph (197 km/h); max. inclined climb, 853 ft/min (4,32 m/sec); hovering ceiling (in ground effect), 5,740 ft (1 750 m); range with six passengers, 375 mls (605 km).
Weights: Empty, 2,403 lb (1 090 kg); max. take-off, 4,960 lb (2 250 kg).
Dimensions: Rotor diam, 36 ft 1¾ in (11,02 m); fuselage length, 32 ft 10¾ in (10,03 m).
Notes: The SA 319 is an Astazou-powered derivative of the Artouste-powered SA 316 Alouette III. All Alouette IIIs built prior to 1970 had the Artouste turboshaft and are now designated SA 316A, the 1970 production model with the Artouste IIIB of 858 shp derated to 543 shp being the SA 316B, and the 1972 model with the Artouste IIID being the SA 316C. The last-mentioned version is manufactured in parallel with the SA 319A, deliveries of which began late in 1970, and the SA 319B with the Astazou XVI was introduced in 1971. Some 1,100 Alouette IIIs had been ordered by the beginning of 1973, and licence production was being under-taken in India, Switzerland, and Rumania.

AÉROSPATIALE SA 321 SUPER FRELON

Country of Origin: France.
Type: Medium transport and multi-purpose helicopter.
Power Plant: Three 1,550 shp Turboméca Turmo III C6 turboshafts.
Performance: Max. speed, 149 mph (240 km/h) at sea level; max. cruise, 143 mph (230 km/h); max. inclined climb, 1,495 ft/min (7,6 m/sec); hovering ceiling (in ground effect), 7,380 ft (2 250 m), (out of ground effect), 1,804 ft (550 m); range with 5,511-lb (2 500-kg) payload and 20 min reserves, 404 mls (650 km).
Weights: Empty, 14,420 lb (6 540 kg); max. take-off, 27,557 lb (12 500 kg).
Dimensions: Rotor diam, 62 ft 0 in (18,90 m); fuselage length, 63 ft 7¾ in (19,40 m).
Notes: Several versions of the Super Frelon (Super Hornet) have been manufactured, including the SA 321G amphibious ASW model for the *Aéronavale* with Sylph radars in outrigger floats, dunking sonar and up to four torpedoes and other ASW stores, the non-amphibious military transport SA 321K (Israel), illustrated above, and SA 321L (South Africa) capable of carrying 27–30 troops or 8,818–9,920 lb (4 000– 4 500 kg) cargo, and the commercial SA 321F (34–37 passenger airliner) and SA 321J heavy-duty utility models. Nine Super Frelons were supplied to the Arab Republic of Libya during 1972.

248

AÉROSPATIALE SA 330 PUMA

Country of Origin: France.
Type: Medium transport helicopter.
Power Plant: Two 1,320 shp Turboméca Turmo III C4 turbo-shafts.
Performance: Max. Speed, 174 mph (280 km/h) at sea level; max. cruise, 165 mph (265 km/h); max. inclined climb, 1,400 ft/min (7,1 m/sec); hovering ceiling (in ground effect), 9,186 ft (2 800 m), (out of ground effect), 6,233 ft (1 900 m); max. range, 390 mls (630 km).
Weights: Empty, 7,561 lb (3 430 kg); max. take-off, 14,110 (6 400 kg).
Dimensions: Rotor diam, 49 ft 2½ on (15,00 m), fuselage length, 46 ft 1½ in (14,06 m).
Notes: The Puma is being built under a joint production agreement between Aérospatiale and Westland, the first to be assembled by the latter concern flying on November 25, 1970. The Puma can accommodate 16–20 troops or up to 5,511 lb (2 500 kg) of cargo, and 40 are being delivered to the RAF for the assault role, 130 having been ordered by French Army Aviation. The Puma has been supplied to the Portuguese, South African, Zaïre Rep., Abu Dhabian, Algerian, and Ivory Coast air arms, and a commercial version, the SA 330F with 1,385 shp Turmo IVA turboshafts, obtained FAA Type Approval in 1971, this carrying 15–17 passengers over 217 mls (350 km).

AÉROSPATIALE SA 341 GAZELLE

Country of Origin: France.
Type: Five-seat light utility helicopter.
Power Plant: One 592 shp Turboméca Astazou IIIN turboshaft.
Performance: Max. speed, 165 mph (265 km/h) at sea level; max. cruise, 149 mph (240 km/h); max. inclined climb rate, 1,214 ft/min (6,16 m/sec); hovering ceiling (in ground effect), 10,170 ft (3 100 m), (out of ground effect), 8,530 ft (2 600 m); max. range, 403 mls (650 km).
Weights: Empty, 1,873 lb (850 kg); max. take-off, 3,747 lb (1 700 kg).
Dimensions: Rotor diam, 34 ft 5½ in (10,50 m); fuselage length, 31 ft 2¾ in (9,52 m).
Notes: Intended as a successor to the Alouette II, the Gazelle is being built under a joint production agreement between Aérospatiale and Westland. Two prototypes and four pre-production Gazelles have flown, and the first production example flew on August 6, 1971. The Gazelle is to be operated in the LOH (Light Observation Helicopter) role by both the French (SA 341F) and British armed forces (SA 341B for the Army, SA 341C for the Navy and SA 341D for the RAF), and it is anticipated that these will respectively purchase some 170 and 250 Gazelles during the first half of the decade. Licence production is to be undertaken in Yugoslavia with deliveries commencing in 1973.

AÉROSPATIALE SA 360

Country of Origin: France.
Type: Multi-purpose and transport helicopter.
Power Plant: One 980 shp Turboméca Astazou XVI turbo-shaft.
Performance: Cruising speed, 161–174 mph (260–280 km/h).
Weights: Empty equipped, 2,866 lb (1 300 kg); max. take-off, 5,510 lb (2 500 kg).
Dimensions: No details available for publication.
Notes: Designed as a successor to the Alouette III and built as a private venture, the SA 360 was flown for the first time on June 2, 1972, but details remained to be revealed by the manufacturer at the time of closing for press. The SA 360 appears to represent a fusion of design features used in the Alouette III and in the later SA 341 Gazelle and, like the latter, employs a ducted tail rotor. Accommodation is provided for two crew members side-by-side with dual controls and eight passengers in two rows on bench-type seats. Plastics are used in the construction of the main rotor blades and much use is made of carbon fibres. The prototype is currently flying with an Astazou XIV turboshaft, but the higher-rated Astazou XVI is expected to be employed by the initial production model with progressively more powerful turboshafts being employed in versions projected for production during the latter half of the present decade.

AGUSTA A 109C HIRUNDO

Country of Origin: Italy.

Type: Eight-seat utility helicopter.

Power Plant: Two 400 shp Allison 250-C20 turboshafts.

Performance: (At 4,850 lb/2 200 kg) Max. speed, 169 mph (272 km/h) at sea level; econ. cruise, 139 mph (223 km/h) at sea level; max. inclined climb, 2,067 ft/min (10,5 m/sec); hovering ceiling (in ground effect), 11,810 ft (3 600 m), (out of ground effect), 9,190 ft (2 800 m); max. range, 457 mls (735 km) at 6,560 ft (2 000 m).

Weights: Empty, 2,645 lb (1 200 kg); max. take-off, 5,291 lb (2 400 kg).

Dimensions: Rotor diam, 36 ft 1 in (11,00 m); fuselage length, 36 ft 7 in (11,14 m).

Notes: The first of four Hirundo (Swallow) prototypes flew on August 4, 1971. This was lost as a result of resonance problems, flight trials being resumed with the second and third prototypes early 1973. The first production examples are scheduled to be delivered late 1973. The Hirundo is intended to fit between the licence-built Bell 206 JetRanger and Bell 212 in the Agusta helicopter range, and carries a pilot and seven passengers in its basic form. It is also suitable for the ambulance role, accommodating two casualty stretchers and two medical attendants when the forward cabin bulkhead is removed, and for freight carrying the forward row of passenger seats may be removed.

BELL MODEL 204B (IROQUOIS)

Country of Origin: USA.

Type: Ten-seat utility helicopter.

Power Plant: One 1,100 shp Lycoming T5311A turboshaft.

Performance: (At 8,500 lb/3 855 kg) Max. speed, 120 mph (193 km/h) at sea level; max. cruise, 110 mph (177 km/h); max. inclined climb, 1,400 ft/min (7,1 m/sec); hovering ceiling (in ground effect), 10,000 ft (3 050 m), (out of ground effect), 4,500 ft (1 370 m); max. range, 392 mls (630 km).

Weights: Empty, 4,600 lb (2 086 kg); max. take-off, 9,500 lb (4 309 kg).

Dimensions: Rotor diam, 48 ft 0 in (14,63 m); fuselage length 40 ft 4⅞ in (12,31 m).

Notes: Licence manufacture of Model 204B undertaken in Italy by Agusta (as AB 204B) and in Japan by Fuji. Variants for US forces include UH-1B and -1C (two crew and seven troops) for US Army, UH-1E (assault support equivalent of of the UH-1C) for the USMC, the UH-1F (missile-site support model with a 1,272 shp General Electric T58-GE-3) and TH-1F (trainer) for the USAF, and the HH-1K (sea-rescue version of the UH-1E with a 1,400 shp Lycoming T53 L-13), TH-1L Seawolf (T53-L-13-powered trainer), and the UH-1L (utility version of the TH-1L) for the US Navy. The AB-204B may have the Gnome H.1200 or T58-GE-3 turboshaft. The Agusta-built ASW version is illustrated.

BELL MODEL 205A (IROQUOIS)

Country of Origin: USA.

Type: Fifteen-seat utility helicopter.

Power Plant: One 1,400 shp Lycoming T5313A turboshaft.

Performance: (At 9,500 lb/4 309 kg) Max. speed, 127 mph (204 km/h) at sea level; max. cruise, 111 mph (179 km/h) at 8,000 ft (2 440 m); max. inclined climb, 1,680 ft/min (8,53 m/sec); hovering ceiling (in ground effect), 10,400 ft (3 170 m), (out of ground effect), 6,000 ft (1 830 m); range, 344 mls (553 km) at 8,000 ft (2 440 m).

Weights: Empty equipped, 5,082 lb (2 305 kg); normal take-off, 9,500 lb (4 309 kg).

Dimensions: Rotor diam, 48 ft 0 in (14,63 m); fuselage length, 41 ft 6 in (12,65 m).

Notes: The Model 205A is basically similar to the Model 204B but introduces a longer fuselage with increased cabin space. It is produced under licence in Italy by Agusta as the AB 205, and is assembled under licence in Formosa (Taiwan). The initial version for the US Army, the UH-1D, has a 1,100 shp T53-L-11 turboshaft. This model was manufactured under licence in Federal Germany. The UH-1D has been succeeded in production for the US Army by the UH-1H (illustrated) with a 1,400 shp T53-L-13 turboshaft, and a similar helicopter for the Mobile Command of the Canadian Armed Forces is designated CUH-1H.

BELL MODEL 206B JETRANGER II

Country of Origin: USA.
Type: Five-seat light utility helicopter.
Power Plant: One 400 shp Allison 250-C20 turboshaft.
Performance: (At 3,000 lb/1 361 kg) Max. cruise, 136 mph (219 km/h) at sea level, 142 mph (228 km/h) at 5,000 ft (1 524 m); hovering ceiling (in ground effect), 13,200 ft (4 023 m), (out of ground effect), 8,700 ft (2 652 m); max. inclined climb, 1,540 ft/min (7,82 m/sec); max. range, 436 mls (702 km) at 10,000 ft (3 048 m).
Weights: Empty, 1,455 lb (660 kg); max. take-off, 3,000 lb (1 360 kg).
Dimensions: Rotor diam, 33 ft 4 in (10,16 m); fuselage length, 31 ft 2 in (9,50 m).
Notes: The JetRanger is manufactured in both commercial and military versions, and the current production variant, the Model 206B JetRanger II, differs from the Model 206A Jet-Ranger in having an uprated turboshaft. A light observation version for the US Army is known as the OH-58A Kiowa, and a training version for the US Navy is known as the TH-57A SeaRanger. An Australian-built version of the Model 206B is being delivered to the Australian Army, and this helicopter is also built in Italy by Agusta as the AB 206B-1. The OH-58A Kiowa has a larger main rotor of 35 ft 4 in (10,77 m) diameter and a fuselage of 32 ft 3½ in (9,84 m) length.

BELL MODEL 209 HUEYCOBRA

Country of Origin: USA.

Type: Two-seat attack helicopter.

Power Plant: (AH-1G) One 1,400 shp Lycoming T53-L-13 turboshaft.

Performance: (AH-1G) Max. speed, 219 mph (352 km/h) at sea level; max. inclined climb, 1,580 ft/min (8 m/sec); hovering ceiling (in ground effect), 9,900 ft (3 015 m); max. range, 387 mls (622 km) at sea level.

Weights: Operational empty, 6,096 lb (2 765 kg); max. take-off, 9,500 lb (4 309 kg).

Dimensions: Rotor diam, 44 ft 0 in (13,41 m); fuselage length, 44 ft 5 in (13,54 m).

Notes: The Model 209 is a development of the UH-1C version of the Model 204B (see page 253) specifically for armed missions. The version for the US Army, the AH-1G (described and illustrated above), has two 7,62-mm Miniguns with 4,000 rpg or two 40-mm grenade launchers with 300 rpg in a forward barbette, and four external stores stations for rockets or gun pods under the stub-wings. The variant for the USMC, the AH-1J SeaCobra, differs from the AH-1G in having a 1,800 shp Pratt & Whitney T400-CP-400 coupled free-turbine turboshaft, a three-barrel 20-mm cannon in the chin barbette, a strengthened tail rotor pylon, and a maximum take-off weight of 10,000 lb (4 535 kg). The AH-1J has been ordered in quantity (202) by Iran.

BELL MODEL 212 TWIN TWO-TWELVE

Country of Origin: USA.

Type: Fifteen-seat utility helicopter.

Power Plant: One 1,800 shp Pratt & Whitney PT6T-3 coupled turboshaft.

Performance: Max. speed, 121 mph (194 km/h) at sea level; max. inclined climb at 10,000 lb (4 535 kg), 1,460 ft/min (7,4 m/sec); hovering ceiling (in ground effect), 17,100 ft (5 212 m), (out of ground effect), 9,900 ft (3 020 m); max. range, 296 mls (476 km) at sea level.

Weights: Empty, 5,500 lb (2 495 kg); max. take-off, 10,000 lb (4 535 kg).

Dimensions: Rotor diam, 48 ft 2½ in (14,69 m); fuselage length, 42 ft 10¾ in (13,07 m).

Notes: The Model 212 is based on the Model 205 (see page 254) from which it differs primarily in having a twin-engined power plant (two turboshaft engines coupled to a combining gearbox with a single output shaft), and both commercial and military versions are being produced. A model for the Canadian Armed Forces is designated CUH-1N, and an essentially similar variant of the Model 212, the UH-1N, is being supplied to the USAF, the USN, and the USMC. All versions of the Model 212 can carry an external load of 4,400 lb (1 814 kg), and can maintain cruise performance on one engine component at maximum gross weight.

BELL MODEL 309 KINGCOBRA

Country of Origin: USA.

Type: Two-seat attack helicopter.

Power Plant: One 1,800 shp Pratt & Whitney T400-CP-400 coupled turboshaft.

Performance: Approx. max. speed, 230 mph (370 km/h); hovering ceiling (out of ground effect), 4,000 ft (1 220 m).

Weights: Max. take-off, 14,000 lb (6 350 kg).

Dimensions: Rotor diam, 49 ft 0 in (14,93 m); fuselage length, 49 ft 0 in (14,93 m).

Notes: The KingCobra is a company-funded development, the first prototype with a T400-CP-400 coupled turboshaft having first flown on September 10, 1971. A second prototype powered by a single 2,850 shp Lycoming T55-L-7C turboshaft commenced its test programme in January 1972. The KingCobra is essentially a growth version of the Model 209 (see page 256) with substantially more power, an enlarged fuselage and a rotor of new design. The first prototype, illustrated above, is fitted with a General Electric chin barbette which can mount either a 20-mm or 30-mm rotary cannon, and the 13-ft (3,96-m) span fixed wing embodies four hardpoints for weapons pylons, a typical underwing load comprising four Hughes TOW missiles and 19 2·75-in (70-mm) rockets beneath each wing. Infra-red, low-light-level television and laser systems are mounted in the nose.

BOEING-VERTOL MODEL 107-II

Country of Origin: USA.

Type: Medium transport helicopter.

Power Plant: Two 1,500 shp General Electric T58-GE-5 turboshafts.

Performance: (At 20,800 lb/9 434 kg) Max. speed, 139 mph (224 km/h); max. inclined climb, 1,920 ft/min (9,75 m/sec); hovering ceiling (in ground effect), 10,000 ft (3 048 m), (out of ground effect), 7,100 ft (2 165 m); range with 2,400 lb (1 088 kg) payload and 30 min reserves, 633 mls (1 020 km).

Weights: Empty equipped, 11,585 lb (5 240 kg); max. take-off, 21,400 lb (9 706 kg).

Dimensions: Rotor diam (each), 50 ft 0 in (15,24 m); fuselage length, 44 ft 10 in (13,66 m).

Notes: The Model 107-II has been in continuous production for military and civil tasks for 11 years, and is licence-manufactured by Kawasaki in Japan for the Air, Ground and Maritime Self-Defence Forces. The specification relates to the latest basic utility model. Versions supplied to the US services comprise the CH-46A (1,250 shp T58-GE-8Bs), CH-46D (1,400 shp T58-GE-10s) and CH-46F (additional electronics) Sea Knight assault transports for the USMC, and the similarly-powered UH-46A and UH-46D Sea Knight utility models for the US Navy. The Model 107-II accommodates three crew and 25 passengers.

BOEING-VERTOL MODEL 114

Country of Origin: USA.
Type: Medium transport helicopter.
Power Plant: (CH-47C) Two 3,750 shp Lycoming T55-L-11 turboshafts.
Performance: (CH-47C at 33,000 lb/14 969 kg) Max. speed, 190 mph (306 km/h) at sea level; average cruise, 158 mph (254 km/h); max. inclined climb, 2,880 ft/min (14,63 m/sec); hovering ceiling (out of ground effect), 14,750 ft (4 495 m); mission radius, 115 mls (185 km).
Weights: Empty, 20,378 lb (9 243); max. take-off, 46,000 lb (20 865 kg).
Dimensions: Rotor diam (each), 60 ft 0 in (18,29 m); fuselage length, 51 ft 0 in (15,54 m).
Notes: The Model 114 is the standard medium transport helicopter of the US Army, and is operated by that service under the designation CH-47 Chinook. The initial production model, the CH-47A, was powered by 2,200 shp T55-L-5 or 2,650 shp T55-L-7 turboshafts. This was succeeded by the CH-47B with 2,850 shp T55-L-7C engines, redesigned rotor blades and other modifications, and this, in turn, gave place to the current CH-47C with more powerful engines, strengthened transmissions, and increased fuel capacity. This model is manufactured in Italy by Elicotteri Meriodionali, orders calling for 26 for the Italian Army and 16 for the Iranian Army (illustrated).

FAIRCHILD 1100

Country of Origin: USA.
Type: Five-seat light utility helicopter.
Power Plant: One 317 shp Allison 250-C18 turboshaft.
Performance: Max. speed, 127 mph (204 km/h) at sea level; econ. cruise, 122 mph (196 km/h); max. inclined climb, 1,600 ft/min (8,1 m/sec); hovering ceiling (in ground effect), 13,400 ft (4 085 m), (out of ground effect), 8,400 ft (2 560 m); range with max. payload, 348 mls (560 km).
Weights: Empty, 1,396 lb (633 kg); max. take-off, 2,750 lb (1 247 kg).
Dimensions: Rotor diam, 35 ft 4¾ in (10,79 m); fuselage length, 29 ft 9½ in (9,08 m).
Notes: The Model 1100 is a refined derivative of the OH-5A which was runner-up in the US Army's first light observation helicopter contest, and the first production model was completed in June 1966. The Model 1100 has since been manufactured in some numbers, primarily for civil duties, and an aeromedical version provides accommodation for two casualty stretchers and a medical attendant. The Model 1100 serves with the Thai Royal Border Police, and is suitable for a variety of military roles. Provision can be made for a wide range of weapons, including torpedoes, depth charges, minigun pods, and rocket launchers, and the Model 1100 has been flown in level flight at 160 mph (257 km/h).

HUGHES MODEL 300

Country of Origin: USA.

Type: Three-seat light utility helicopter.

Power Plant: (Model 300C) One 190 shp Lycoming HIO-360-D1A four-cylinder horizontally-opposed engine.

Performance: (Model 300C) Max. speed, 105 mph (169 km/h); max. cruise, 100 mph (161 km/h) at 5,000 ft (1 525 m); max. inclined climb, 1,100 ft/min (5,08 m/sec); hovering ceiling (in ground effect), 7,600 ft (2 316 m), (out of ground effect), 5,200 ft (1 585 m); max. range, 255 mls (410 km).

Weights: Empty, 1,025 lb (465 kg); max. take-off, 1,900 lb (861 kg).

Dimensions: Rotor diam, 26 ft 10 in (8,18 m); fuselage length, 23 ft 1 in (7,03 m).

Notes: Originally developed as the Model 269B, the Model 300 has been in continuous production since 1963, and 792 examples of this light helicopter have been supplied to the US Army for the primary training role as the TH-55A. The current production version, the Model 300C described by the specification, differs from the basic Model 300 (which was powered by a 180 hp Lycoming HIO-360-A1A) in having a more powerful engine, main and tail rotors of increased diameter, and structural changes including a lengthened tail boom and a taller rotor mast. Deliveries of the Model 300C commenced in 1970.

HUGHES MODEL 500

Country of Origin: USA.

Type: Six-seat light utility helicopter.

Power Plant: One 317 shp Allison 250-C18A turboshaft.

Performance: Max. speed, 152 mph (244 km/h) at 1,000 ft (305 m); range cruise, 138 mph (222 km/h) at sea level; max. inclined climb, 1,700 ft/min (8,64 m/sec); hovering ceiling (in ground effect), 8,200 ft (2 500 m), (out of ground effect), 5,300 ft (1 615 m); max. range, 377 mls (589 km) at 4,000 ft (1 220 m).

Weights: Empty, 1,086 lb (492 kg); max. take-off, 2,550 lb (1 157 kg).

Dimensions: Rotor diam, 26 ft 4 in (8,03 m); fuselage length, 23 ft 0 in (7,01 m).

Notes: The Model 500 (also known by the engineering designation Model 369) is being manufactured for both commercial and foreign military use, the military configuration being known as the Model 500M. Both Models 500 and 500M have been assembled in Italy by Nardi which began licence manufacture during 1971, and licence manufacture is also being undertaken by Kawasaki in Japan. The current Model 500 is essentially similar to the OH-6A Cayuse light observation helicopter for the US Army, but its turboshaft is only derated to 278 shp (as compared with 252 shp for the Allison T63-A-5A of the OH-6A), and internal volume and fuel capacity are increased.

KAMAN HH-2 SEASPRITE

Country of Origin: USA.

Type: All-weather search and rescue helicopter.

Power Plant: Two 1,250 shp General Electric T58-GE-8B turboshafts.

Performace: (HH-2D) Max. speed, 168 mph (270 km/h) at sea level; normal cruise, 152 mph (245 km/h); max. inclined climb, 2,540 ft/min (12,9 m/sec); hovering ceiling (in ground effect), 16,900 ft (5 150 m), (out of ground effect), 14,100 ft (4 300 m); max. range, 425 mls (685 km).

Weights: (HH-2D) Empty, 7,500 lb (3 401 kg); normal take-off, 10,187 lb (4 620 kg); max. overload, 12,500 lb (5 670 kg).

Dimensions: Rotor diam, 44 ft 0 in (13,41 m); fuselage length, 37 ft 8 in (11,48 m).

Notes: The HH-2C and HH-2D are specialised search and rescue conversions of the single-engined UH-2A and -2B multi-role versions of the Seasprite (see 1966 edition), and, like the UH-2C (see 1969 edition), are modified to twin-engined configuration. The HH-2C is an armed and armoured model with a chin-mounted Minigun barbette and waist-mounted machine guns, and the HH-2D is similar but lacks armour and armament. The HH-2D differs from the UH-2C in having a four-bladed tail rotor, dual main-wheels, and uprated transmission, and the SH-2D (illustrated) is an adaptation for anti-submarine warfare and missile defence.

KAMOV KA-25K (HORMONE)

Country of Origin: USSR.

Type: Utility and flying crane helicopter.

Power Plant: Two 900 shp Glushenkov GTD-3 turboshafts.

Performance: Max. speed, 137 mph (220 km/h); normal cruise, 121 mph (195 km/h); range with max. payload, 248 mls (400 km), with max. fuel, 404 mls (650 km); service ceiling, 10,670 ft (3 250 m).

Weights: Empty, 9,259 lb (4 200 kg); normal take-off, 15,653 lb (7 100 kg); max. take-off, 16,094 lb (7 300 kg).

Dimensions: Rotor diam (each), 51 ft 7½ in (15,74 m); fuselage length, 34 ft 3 in (10,44 m).

Notes: Derived from and developed in parallel with the Ka-25 shipboard ASW helicopter (see page 266), the Ka-25K utility and flying crane helicopter was flown in prototype form in 1965, and features an aft-facing glazed gondola beneath the fuselage nose accommodating a winch operator, the gondola containing a dual set of controls. The main cabin, normally used for freight, can accommodate 12 passengers on folding seats. Each wheel may be enclosed by an inflatable pontoon, and the rotors, transmission and engines with their auxiliaries form a single self-contained assembly which may be removed within one hour. The Ka-25K is claimed to combine good manœuvrability and minimum dimensions with a high payload-to-AUW ratio.

KAMOV KA-25 (HORMONE A)

Country of Origin: USSR.
Type: Shipboard anti-submarine warfare helicopter.
Power Plant: Two 900 shp Glushenkov GTD-3 turboshafts.
Performance: (Estimated) Max. speed, 130 mph (209 km/h); normal cruise, 120 mph (193 km/h); max. range, 400 mls (644 km); service ceiling, 11,000 ft (3 353 m).
Weights: (Estimated) Empty, 10,500 lb (4 765 kg); max. take-off, 16,500 lb (7 484 kg).
Dimensions: Rotor diam (each), 51 ft 7½ in (15,74 m); approx. fuselage length, 35 ft 6 in (10,82 m).
Notes: Possessing a basically similar airframe to that of the Ka-25K (see page 265) and employing a similar self-contained assembly comprising rotors, transmission, engines and auxiliaries, the Ka-25 serves with the Soviet Navy primarily in the ASW role but is also employed in the utility and transport roles. The ASW Ka-25 serves aboard the helicopter cruisers *Moskva* and *Leningrad* as well as with shore-based units. A search radar installation is mounted in a nose radome, but other sensor housings and antennae differ widely from helicopter to helicopter. There is no evidence that externally-mounted weapons may be carried. Each landing wheel is surrounded by an inflatable pontoon surmounted by inflation bottles. Sufficient capacity is available to accommodate up to a dozen personnel.

KAMOV KA-26 (HOODLUM)

Country of Origin: USSR.

Type: Light utility helicopter.

Power Plant: Two 325 shp Vedeneev M-14V-26 air-cooled radial engines.

Performance: Max. speed, 106 mph (170 km/h); max. cruise, 93 mph (150 km/h); econ. cruise, 56 mph (90 km/h) at 9,840 ft (3 000 m); hovering ceiling at 6,615 lb (3 000 kg) (in ground effect), 4,265 ft (1 300 m), (out of ground effect), 2,625 ft (800 m); range with seven passengers and 30 min reserves, 248 mls (400 km).

Weights: Empty (stripped), 4,300 lb (1 950 kg), (with passenger pod), 4,630 lb (2 100 kg); max. take-off, 7,165 lb (3 250 kg).

Dimensions: Rotor diam (each), 42 ft 8 in (13,00 m); fuselage length, 25 ft 5 in (7,75 m).

Notes: Flown for the first time in 1965, and placed in large-scale production during the following year, the Ka-26 was designed from the outset to carry interchangeable pods for freight or passengers, a chemical hopper with spraybars or dust-spreader, an open freight platform, or a hook for slung loads. The passenger-carrying pod can accommodate up to six passengers, and in the aeromedical role the Ka-26 can carry two casualty stretchers, two seated casualties and a medical attendant.

MBB BO 105

Country of Origin: Federal Germany.
Type: Five/six-seat light utility helicopter.
Power Plant: Two 400 shp Allison 250-C20 turboshafts.
Performance: Max. speed, 155 mph (250 km/h) at sea level; max. cruise, 138 mph (222 km/h); max. inclined climb, 1,870 ft/min (9,5 m/sec); hovering ceiling (in ground effect), 7,610 ft (2 320 m), (out of ground effect), 5,085 ft (1 550 m); normal range, 388 mls (625 km) at 5,000 ft (1 525 m).
Weights: Empty, 2,360 lb (1 070 kg); normal take-off, 4,630 lb (2 100 kg); max. take-off, 5,070 lb (2 300 kg).
Dimensions: Rotor diam, 32 ft 1¾ in (9,80 m); fuselage length, 28 ft 0½ in (8,55 m).
Notes: The BO 105 features a rigid unarticulated main rotor with folding glass-fibre reinforced plastic blades, and the first prototype (with a conventional rotor) was tested in 1966, three prototypes being followed by four pre-production examples, and production deliveries commencing during 1971. The German armed forces are acquiring six examples for evaluation, and US manufacturing rights have been acquired by Boeing Vertol. The third prototype was powered by 375 shp MTU 6022 turboshafts, but the production model has standardised on the Allison 250. Production is undertaken by the Siebelwerke-ATG subsidiary of MBB.

MIL MI-2 (HOPLITE)

Country of Origin: USSR.

Type: Light general-purpose helicopter.

Power Plant: Two 437 shp Izotov GTD-350 turboshafts.

Performance: Max. speed, 130 mph (210 km/h) at 1,640 ft (500 m); max. cruise, 124 mph (200 km/h); econ. cruise, 118 mph (190 km/h); max. inclined climb, 885 ft/min (4,5 m/sec); hovering ceiling (in ground effect), 6,550 ft (2 000 m), (out of ground effect), 3,275 ft (1 000 m); range with max. payload and 5% reserves, 105 mls (170 km), with max. fuel and 30 min reserves, 360 mls (580 km).

Weights: Operational empty, 5,180 lb (2 350 kg); normal take-off, 7,826 lb (3 550 kg); overload take-off, 8,157 lb (3 700 kg).

Dimensions: Rotor diam, 47 ft 6¾ in (14,50 m); fuselage length, 37 ft 4¼ in (11,40 m).

Notes: After completion of prototype development in the Soviet Union, production and marketing of the Mi-2 were transferred to Poland where manufacture of this helicopter (at the WSK-Swidnik) has been undertaken since 1966. The Mi-2 has been built in large numbers for both civil and military tasks, and has been exported widely. Accommodation may be provided for a single pilot and six to eight passengers or up to 1,543 lb (700 kg) of freight. Four casualty stretchers and a medical attendant can be carried.

269

MIL MI-6 (HOOK)

Country of Origin: USSR.

Type: Heavy transport helicopter.

Power Plant: Two 5,500 shp Soloviev D-25V turboshafts.

Performance: (At 93,700 lb/42 500 kg) Max. speed, 186 mph (300 km/h); max. cruise, 155 mph (250 km/h); service ceiling, 14,750 ft (4 500 m); range with 17,640-lb (8 000-kg) payload, 385 mls (620 km), with 9,920-lb (4 500-kg) payload and external tanks, 620 mls (1 000 km).

Weights: Empty, 60,055 lb (27 240 kg); normal take-off, 89,285 lb (40 500 kg); max. take-off (for VTO), 93,700 lb (42 500 kg).

Dimensions: Rotor diam, 114 ft 10 in (35,00 m); fuselage length, 108 ft 9½ in (33,16 m).

Notes: First flown in 1957, the Mi-6 has been built in very large numbers for both civil and military roles. With a crew of five, the Mi-6 can accommodate 65 passengers or 41 casualty stretchers and two medical attendants, and clam-shell-type doors and folding ramps facilitate the loading of vehicles and bulky freight. Two heavy flying-crane helicopters have been evolved from the Mi-6, the Mi-10 (see 1966 edition) flown in 1961 and the Mi-10K (see 1970 edition) flown in 1965, these being almost identical to the Mi-6 above the line of the cabin. The Mi-6 has been supplied to the armed forces of North Vietnam, Egypt and Indonesia.

MIL MI-8 (HIP)

Country of Origin: USSR.
Type: General-purpose transport helicopter.
Power Plant: Two 1,500 shp Izotov TB-2-117A turboshafts.
Performance: (At 24,470 lb/11 100 kg) Max. speed, 155 mph (250 km/h); max. cruise, 140 mph (225 km/h); hovering ceiling (in ground effect), 5,900 ft (1 800 m), (out of ground effect), 2,625 ft (800 m); service ceiling, 14,760 ft (4 500 m); range with 6,615 lb (3 000 kg) of freight, 264 mls (425 km).
Weights: Empty (cargo), 15,787 lb (7 171 kg), (passenger), 16,352 lb (7 417 kg); normal take-off, 24,470 lb (11 100 kg); max. take-off (for VTO), 26,455 lb (12 000 kg).
Dimensions: Rotor diam, 69 ft 10¼ in (21,29 m); fuselage length, 59 ft 7⅓ in (18,17 m).
Notes: The Mi-8 has been in continuous production since 1964 for both civil and military tasks. The standard commercial passenger version has a basic flight crew of two or three and 28 four-abreast seats, and the aeromedical version accommodates 12 casualty stretchers and a medical attendant. As a freighter the Mi-8 will carry up to 8,818 lb (4 000 kg) of cargo, and military tasks include assault transport, search and rescue, and anti-submarine warfare. The Mi-8 is now operated by several Warsaw Pact air forces, serving primarily in the support transport role.

MIL MI-12 (HOMER)

Country of Origin: USSR.

Type: Heavy transport helicopter.

Power Plant: Four 6,500 shp Soloviev D-25VF turboshafts.

Performance: Max. speed, 161 mph (260 km/h); cruise, 149 mph (240 km/h); range with max. payload of 78,000 lb (35 380 kg), 310 mls (500 km); service ceiling, 11,500 ft (3 500 m).

Weights: Normal take-off, 213,848 lb (97 000 kg); max. take-off, 231,485 lb (105 000 kg).

Dimensions: Rotor diam (each), 114 ft 9$\frac{1}{2}$ in (35,00 m); fuselage length, 121 ft 4 in (37,00 m).

Notes: First flown in the autumn of 1968 and currently the world's largest helicopter, the Mi-12 carries a crew of six of which the pilot, co-pilot, flight engineer and electrician are accommodated on the lower flight deck with the navigator and radio-operator on the upper deck. The Mi-12 employs the dynamic components of the Mi-6 (see page 270), being in effect two Mi-6 power units, main transmissions and main rotors mounted side-by-side at the tips of braced wings, the overall width with the rotors turning being 219 ft 9 in (67,00 m). The Mi-12 was evidently designed to carry loads compatible with those carried by the fixed-wing An-22 transport, and three prototypes have been built. Production was expected to commence during the course of 1972 for both the Soviet Air Forces and *Aeroflot*.

SIKORSKY S-58T

Country of Origin: USA.

Type: General-purpose transport helicopter.

Power Plant: One 1,525 shp Pratt & Whitney PT6T-3 coupled turboshaft.

Performance: Max. speed, 123 mph (198 km/h) at sea level; max. cruise, 115 mph (185 km/h); econ. cruise, 92 mph (148 km/h); hovering ceiling (out of ground effect), 6,500 ft (1 980 m); max. range, 480 mls (772 km).

Weights: Empty, 7,300 lb (3 311 kg); max. take-off, 13,000 lb (5 896 kg).

Dimensions: Rotor diam, 56 ft 0 in (17,07 m); fuselage length, 47 ft 3 in (14,4 m).

Notes: The S-58T is a turbine-powered conversion of the piston-engined S-58, affording improved performance, lower operating costs and increased reliability. Design of the S-58T conversion commenced in January 1970, and the prototype conversion was first flown on August 19, 1970. A number of used S-58s have been obtained by Sikorsky Aircraft and are being offered for sale after conversion to turbine power, and the company is also producing retrofit kits to enable S-58 operators to convert their own helicopters to S-58T standards. A total of 40 converted helicopters and conversion kits had been sold by the beginning of 1973. The S-58T has a normal flight crew of two with dual controls, and can accommodate 12–16 passengers.

SIKORSKY S-61A

Country of Origin: USA.

Type: Amphibious transport and rescue helicopter.

Power Plant: (S-61A-4) Two 1,500 shp General Electric T58-GE-5 turboshafts.

Performance: (At 20,500 lb/9 300 kg) Max. speed, 153 mph (248 km/h); range cruise, 126 mph (203 km/h); max. inclined climb, 2,200 ft/min (11,17 m/sec); hovering ceiling (in ground effect), 8,600 ft (2 820 m); range with max. fuel and 10 % reserves, 525 mls (845 km).

Weights: Empty, 9,763 lb (4 428 kg); normal take-off, 20,500 lb (9 300 kg); max., 21,500 lb (9 750 kg).

Dimensions: Rotor diam, 62 ft 0 in (18,90 m); fuselage length, 54 ft 9 in (16,69 m).

Notes: A transport equivalent of the S-61B (see page 283) with sonar, weapons, and automatic blade folding deleted, and a cargo floor inserted, the S-61A is used by the USAF for missile site support as the CH-3B, this having 1,250 shp T58-GE-8Bs and accommodation for 26 troops or 15 stretchers. Eight similarly-powered S-61A-1s supplied to Denmark for the rescue task were supplemented in 1970 by a ninth machine, and 10 T58-GE-5-powered S-61A-4s equipped to carry 31 combat troops and supplied to Malaysia were supplemented during 1971 by six further S-61A-4s. The S-61L and S-61N (see 1967 edition) are non-amphibious and amphibious commercial versions.

274

SIKORSKY S-61R

Country of Origin: USA.

Type: Amphibious transport and rescue helicopter.

Power Plant: (CH-3E) Two 1,500 shp General Electric T58-GE-5 turboshafts.

Performance: (CH-3E at 21,247 lb/9 635 kg) Max. speed, 162 mph (261 km/h) at sea level; range cruise, 144 mph (232 km/h); max. inclined climb, 1,310 ft/min (6,6 m/sec); hovering ceiling (in ground effect), 4,100 ft (1 250 m); range with 10% reserves, 465 mls (748 km).

Weights: (CH-3E) Empty, 13,255 lb (6 010 kg); normal take-off, 21,247 lb (9 635 kg); max. take-off, 22,050 lb (10 000 kg).

Dimensions: Rotor diam, 62 ft 0 in (18,90 m); fuselage length, 57 ft 3 in (17,45 m).

Notes: Although based on the S-61A, the S-61R embodies numerous design changes, including a rear ramp and a tricycle-type undercarriage. Initial model for the USAF was the CH-3C with 1,300 shp T58-GE-1 turboshafts, but this was subsequently updated to CH-3E standards. The CH-3E can accommodate 25–30 troops or 5,000 lb (2 270 kg) of cargo, and may be fitted with a TAT-102 barbette on each sponson mounting a 7,62-mm Minigun. The HH-3E is a USAF rescue version with armour, self-sealing tanks, and refuelling probe, and the HH-3F Pelican (illustrated) is a US Coast Guard search and rescue model.

SIKORSKY S-62A

Country of Origin: USA.

Type: Amphibious utility transport helicopter.

Power Plant: One 1,250 shp General Electric CT58-110-1 turboshaft.

Performance: Max. speed, 101 mph (163 km/h) at sea level; max. cruise, 92 mph (148 km/h); max. inclined climb, 1,140 ft/min (5,8 m/sec); hovering ceiling (in ground effect), 14,100 ft (4 295 m), (out of ground effect), 4,600 ft (1 400 m); range with 10% reserves, 462 mls (743 km).

Weights: Empty equipped, 4,957 lb (2 248 kg); max. take-off, 7,900 lb (3 583 kg).

Dimensions: Rotor diam, 53 ft 0 in (16,16 m); fuselage length, 44 ft 6½ in (13,58 m).

Notes: The S-62 embodies many components of the piston-engined S-55 (see 1961 edition), including rotor blades and heads, and the basic model is the S-62A which can accommodate 12 troops or 10 airline passengers. The S-62A is licence-built in Japan by Mitsubishi for both military and civil roles, both the Maritime and Air Self-Defence Forces using this type in the rescue role. A US Coast Guard rescue version is designated HH-52A (see 1970 edition), this having a rescue platform, and automatic stabilisation and towing equipment. The HH-52A operates at higher weights, the S-62C being the commercial and military foreign version.

SIKORSKY S-64 SKYCRANE

Country of Origin: USA.

Type: Heavy flying-crane helicopter.

Power Plant: Two 4,500 shp Pratt & Whitney T73-P-1 turboshafts.

Performance: (CH-54A at 38,000 lb/17 237 kg) Max. speed, 127 mph (204 km/h) at sea level; max. cruise, 109 mph (175 km/h); max. inclined climb, 1,700 ft/min (8,64 m/sec); hovering ceiling (in ground effect), 10,600 ft (3 230 m), (out of ground effect), 6,900 ft (2 100 m); range, 253 mls (407 km).

Weights: (CH-54A) Empty, 19,234 lb (8 724 kg); max. take-off, 42,000 lb (19 050 kg).

Dimensions: Rotor diam, 72 ft 0 in (21,95 m); fuselage length, 70 ft 3 in (21,41 m).

Notes: The S-64A serves with the US Army as the CH-54A Tarhe in the heavy lift role, and may be fitted with a 15,000-lb (6 800-kg) hoist or an all-purpose pod (seen fitted above) which can accommodate 45 troops or 24 casualty stretchers. The commercial equivalent of the CH-54A is designated S-64E. A developed version, the CH-54B powered by T73-P-700 turboshafts of 4,800 shp, was flown on June 30, 1969, other changes including dual mainwheels and an increase in max. take-off to 47,000 lb (21 319 kg). The CH-54B also features a new gearbox and high-lift rotor blades, the civil equivalent being the S-64F.

SIKORSKY S-65

Country of Origin: USA.

Type: Heavy assault transport helicopter.

Power Plant: Two 3,925 shp General Electric T64-GE-413 turboshafts.

Performance: Max. speed, 196 mph (315 km/h) at sea level; max. cruise, 173 mph (278 km/h); max. inclined climb, 2,180 ft/min (11,08 m/sec); hovering ceiling (in ground effect), 13,400 ft (4 080 m), (out of ground effect), 6,500 ft (1 980 m); range, 257 mls (413 km).

Weights: Empty, 23,485 lb (10 653 kg); normal take-off, 36,400 lb (16 510 kg); 42,000 lb (19 050 kg).

Dimensions: Rotor diam, 72 ft 3 in (22,02 m); fuselage length, 67 ft 2 in (20,47 m).

Notes: Using many components based on those of the S-64 (see page 277), the S-65 can accommodate 38 combat troops or 24 casualty stretchers and four medical attendants. The initial US Navy version, the CH-53A Sea Stallion, has 2,850 shp T64-GE-6 turboshafts, and the HH-53B for the USAF is similar apart from having 3,080 shp T64-GE-3s, a flight refuelling probe, jettisonable auxiliary tanks and armament, the HH-53C differing primarily in having 3,435 shp T64-GE-7s and an external cargo hook. The US Marine Corps' CH-53D (to which the specification applies) has up-rated engines and can carry up to 64 troops. The CH-53DG for Germany (illustrated) and S-65-Oe for Austria are similar.

SIKORSKY S-67 BLACKHAWK

Country of Origin: USA.
Type: Two-seat attack helicopter.
Power Plant: Two 1,530 shp General Electric T58/T5A1A turboshafts.
Performance: Max. speed, 218 mph (351 km/h); mission endurance (with 12,997 lb/5 897 kg armament payload), 1 hr, (with full internal fuel and 7,350 lb/3 333 kg armament payload), 2·7 hr; ferry range (with 1,250 Imp gal/5 682 l external fuel), 1,730 mls (2 784 km) at 173 mph (278 km/h).
Weights: Max. take-off, 28,000 lb (12 700 kg).
Dimensions: Rotor diam, 62 ft 0 in (18,90 m); fuselage length, 64 ft 9 in (19,74 m).
Notes: The S-67 is a company-funded development based on the unsuccessful S-66 entry in the US Army's AAFSS (Advanced Aerial Fire Support System) competition, and rotors, gearboxes, drive shafts, and controls are similar to those of the S-61. A TAT-140 gun barbette beneath the forward fuselage mounts a 30-mm multi-barrel cannon with 1,500 rounds, laser ranging and IR target designation. Six external weapons points can lift up to 11,800 lb (5 352 kg) of offensive stores. Although the US Army has now specified a smaller gunship helicopter and is unlikely to procure a type as large as the Blackhawk, development was proceeding at the beginning of 1973.

D-9543

VFW-FOKKER H3 SPRINTER

Country of Origin: Federal Germany.

Type: Three-seat light compound helicopter.

Power Plant: One 400 hp Allison 250-C20 turboshaft.

Performance: Max. cruise, 155 mph (250 km/h) at sea level; inclined climb, 1,280 ft/min (6,5 m/sec); hovering ceiling (in ground effect), 5,070 ft (1 540 m), (out of ground effect), 1,500 ft (455 m); max. range, 490 mls (790 km).

Weights: Empty, 1,090 lb (495 kg); max. take-off, 2,134 lb (968 kg).

Dimensions: Rotor diam. 28 ft 6½ in (8,70 m); fuselage length, 24 ft 2¼ in (7,37 m).

Notes: The H3 Sprinter was flown for the first time on March 15, 1971, and is intended to be the first in a family of compound helicopters currently planned by VFW-Fokker. The three-blade rotor is tip-driven by compressed air for vertical take-off, hovering and landing, and for transition to forward flight power is progressively transferred to two shrouded seven-bladed airscrews mounted on stub fairings on the fuselage sides. These were not fitted for initial flight trials (as illustrated). In horizontal flight the rotor autorotates, eliminating the need for conventional transmission and drive-shaft systems, hydraulic systems, clutches and torque compensation. In the event of an engine failure full rotor autorotation is maintained.

280

WESTLAND WASP

Country of Origin: United Kingdom.
Type: Five/six-seat general-purpose and anti-submarine warfare helicopter.
Power Plant: One 710 shp Rolls-Royce Bristol Nimbus 503 turboshaft.
Performance: Max. speed, 120 mph (193 km/h) at sea level; max. cruise, 110 mph (177 km/h); max. inclined climb, 1,440 ft/min (7,4 m/sec); hovering ceiling (in ground effect), 12,500 ft (3 810 m), (out of ground effect), 8,800 ft (2 682 m); max. range with standard fuel, 303 mls (488 km).
Weights: Empty, 3,452 lb (1 566 kg); max. take-off, 5,500 lb (2 495 kg).
Dimensions: Rotor diam, 32 ft 3 in (9,83 m); fuselage length, 30 ft 4 in (9,24 m).
Notes: In its H.A.S. Mk. 1 form, the Wasp serves with the Royal Navy in the anti-submarine weapon-carrying role, operating from platforms aboard frigates equipped with long-range asdic. In this role the Wasp is normally crewed by a single pilot and carries two 270-lb (122,4-kg) torpedoes. Dual controls may be fitted. The Wasp has been supplied to the Brazilian (3), New Zealand (12), Netherlands (12) and South African (10) navies, and the production line was re-opened in 1972 to fulfil a supplementary order from South Africa for a further seven helicopters of this type.

WESTLAND WG.13 LYNX

Country of Origin: United Kingdom.

Type: Multi-purpose and transport helicopter.

Power Plant: Two 900 shp Rolls-Royce BS.360-07-26 turboshafts.

Performance: (General purpose versions) Max. speed, 207 mph (333 km/h); max. cruise, 184 mph (296 km/h) at sea level; max. inclined climb, 2,800 ft/min (14,2 m/sec); hovering ceiling (out of ground effect), 12,000 ft (3 650 m); range (with 10 passengers), 173 mls (278 km), (with internal cargo and full tanks), 489 mls (788 km).

Weights: Operational empty, 5,532–6,125 lb (2 509–2 778 kg); max. take-off, 8,000 lb (3 620 kg); overload, 8,840 lb (4 009 kg).

Dimensions: Rotor diam, 42 ft 0 in (12,80 m); fuselage length, 38 ft 3¼ in (11,66 m).

Notes: The Lynx, the first of 12 prototypes of which commenced its flight test programme on March 21, 1971, and the first production machine (a Lynx A.H. Mk. 1 for the British Army) is scheduled to fly at the end of 1973 with the first naval example (a Lynx HR Mk. 2 for the Royal Navy) following mid-1974. Current plans call for the delivery of some 80 examples of an ASW version to France's *Aéronavale*, the Lynx being one of three helicopter types covered by the Anglo-French agreement. A total of 277 is programmed for the British services.

285

286